TRACE EVIDENCE

Titles in the True Forensic Crime Stories series:

BONES
DEAD PEOPLE DO TELL TALES
Library Ed. ISBN 978-0-7660-3669-7
Paperback ISBN 978-1-59845-363-8

CYBERCRIME
DATA TRAILS DO TELL TALES
Library Ed. ISBN 978-0-7660-3668-0
Paperback ISBN 978-1-59845-361-4

DNA AND BLOOD
DEAD PEOPLE DO TELL TALES
Library Ed. ISBN 978-0-7660-3667-3
Paperback ISBN 978-1-59845-362-1

FINGERPRINTS
DEAD PEOPLE DO TELL TALES
Library Ed. ISBN 978-0-7660-3689-5
Paperback ISBN 978-1-59845-364-5

GUN CRIMES
DEAD PEOPLE DO TELL TALES
Library Ed. ISBN 978-0-7660-3763-2
Paperback ISBN 978-1-59845-365-2

TRACE EVIDENCE
DEAD PEOPLE DO TELL TALES
Library Ed. ISBN 978-0-7660-3664-2
Paperback ISBN 978-1-59845-366-9

TRACE EVIDENCE

Dead People DO Tell tales

Stephen Eldridge

Enslow Publishers, Inc.
40 Industrial Road
Box 398
Berkeley Heights, NJ 07922
USA
http://www.enslow.com

This book, and everything else, is dedicated to my wife, Ali.

Library of Congress Cataloging-in-Publication Data
Eldridge, Stephen.
 Trace evidence : dead people do tell tales / Stephen Eldridge.
  p. cm. — (True forensic crime stories)
 Includes bibliographical references and index.
 Summary: "Uses true crime stories to explain the science of forensics and trace evidence"
—Provided by publisher.
 ISBN 978-0-7660-3664-2
 1. Forensic sciences—Juvenile literature. I. Title.
 HV8073.8.E43 2012
 363.25'62—dc22
                    2010001117

Paperback ISBN 978-1-59845-366-9

Printed in China

052011 Leo Paper Group, Heshan City, Guangdong, China

10 9 8 7 6 5 4 3 2 1

To Our Readers: We have done our best to make sure all Internet Addresses in this book were active
and appropriate when we went to press. However, the author and the publisher have no control over
and assume no liability for the material available on those Internet sites or on other Web sites they
may link to. Any comments or suggestions can be sent by e-mail to comments@enslow.com or to the
address on the back cover.

Photo Credits: Associated Press, pp. 35, 48, 52, 71, 82; Hulton Archive/Getty Images, p. 9;
© Mikael Karlsson/Alamy, p. 61; Photo Researchers, Inc.: BSIP, p. 43, Cheryl Power, p. 15, David
R. Frazier, p. 41, Dr. Jurgen Scriba, p. 44, Eye of Science, p. 24, Gary S. Settles, p. 84, Louise Murray,
p. 54, Lauren Shear, p. 66, Mauro Fermariello, pp. 17, 31, 74, Peter Menzel, p. 86; Shutterstock.com,
pp. 1, 3, 5, 6, 11, 13, 18, 20, 22, 34–35, 58, 68, 69, 78, 79, 80.

Cover Photos: Shutterstock.com

Contents

7 CHAPTER 1: Putting Pieces Together

19 CHAPTER 2: Combing for Evidence

29 CHAPTER 3: Not Quite Spotless

38 CHAPTER 4: When Is Trace Evidence Meaningful?

50 CHAPTER 5: Piling on the Evidence

59 CHAPTER 6: Vanished With a Trace

70 CHAPTER 7: The Math Behind the Science

81 CHAPTER 8: Serving Justice

90 CAREERS

92 CHAPTER NOTES

98 GLOSSARY

100 FURTHER READING AND INTERNET ADDRESSES

102 INDEX

The fictional detective Sherlock Holmes solved crimes by examining evidence very carefully, sometimes with a magnifying glass.

Putting Pieces Together

"I am glad of all details, whether they seem to you to be relevant or not."[1] These are the words of the famous fictional detective Sherlock Holmes. He shows that sometimes small things that seem unimportant can provide valuable evidence in solving crimes. Holmes may be the first character to specialize in catching criminals by examining tiny clues.[2] He studies a crime scene with a magnifying glass. He believes that every detail can tell him something about the crime and the criminal who committed it. Holmes has become famous because of his painstaking analysis of every detail of a crime.

Sherlock Holmes was a character in the stories of Sir Arthur Conan Doyle. Although he does not really exist, he is an inspiration for real detectives and investigators. In the first Sherlock Holmes story, Holmes discovers a body and a scrap of writing that contains a single mysterious word. Holmes solves the crime due to his amazing detective skills.

HANS GROSS

HANS GROSS WAS AN Austrian criminologist who lived around the same time that Sir Arthur Conan Doyle was writing about Sherlock Holmes. Gross was a professor who composed some of the first rules for how investigators should behave at a crime scene. Gross and Holmes had a similar approach to detection. Gross believed that the most important thing for an investigator was to "observe absolute calm."[4] The idea was to never move or in any way touch anything at the scene of a crime before it could be described or photographed for the record. In Gross's view, like Holmes's, nothing is too small to be important to an investigation.

However, Holmes himself once said, "Life is infinitely stranger than anything which the mind of man could invent."[3]

Unlike Sherlock Holmes, Eugène François Vidocq was a real detective. Despite this, Vidocq was almost certainly a stranger character than Holmes! As a young man in the late 1700s, Vidocq was a criminal. He was a thief and a deserter who had run away from the French army. When he grew older, though, he decided to turn his life around. First, he became a spy for the police. Eventually, he was made a police officer, even becoming the head of one of the first groups of police detectives in the world. Vidocq's methods sound like they come from movies or television, but they were real. He used disguises to infiltrate criminal organizations. He employed other former criminals, including some that worked for him in secret. He had an amazing memory that allowed him to easily recognize any criminal he'd seen before. He even started his own detective agency—maybe the first in the world. He used traces—small clues—at crime scenes to solve crimes, decades before Sir Arthur Conan Doyle first wrote about Sherlock Holmes.

The cover of a book about Eugène François
Vidocq, a famous real-life detective

Suppose you are Eugène François Vidocq and it is the beginning of the nineteenth century. A man named Fontaine has been stabbed. He has twenty-eight wounds, and at first you believe he is dead. He is taken away to be examined—but he is still alive. He is even able to tell you what happened to him. He was attacked by two men. The attackers stabbed him and robbed him. Fontaine fought back, and one of the men was hurt in the struggle. Despite the injury, the criminals got away. Fontaine does not know who the men who robbed him were, and no one else saw the crime.[5]

How do you solve such a case? If you are Vidocq, you begin with **trace evidence**.

Forensic Science

The case of Mr. Fontaine involves **forensic science**. Forensic science is the process of using clues and evidence to solve crimes. Because there are many kinds of clues, forensic scientists may use many different scientific fields (such as physics, chemistry, and biology) to help crack a case. Paul L. Kirk, an American forensic scientist, explained forensic analysis this way: "Wherever [a criminal] steps, whatever he touches, whatever he leaves, even unconsciously, will serve as a silent witness against him."[6] It is almost impossible for criminals to act without leaving a trace. Wherever people go, they may shed one of the millions of hairs on their bodies. They may mark anything they touch with fingerprints. They may leave footprints with every step. Forensic scientists find those traces—called trace evidence—and use them to catch criminals.

Trace evidence can take almost any form. According to one trace analyst, "Trace involves everything. And every case is different. Even if it's two shoe print cases, they're different. One might be in mud. The next one might be on a piece of paper. One might be in blood. Every case is different."[7] Trace analysts have to be knowledgeable in many different

FINGERPRINTS

Maybe the most famous kind of trace evidence is fingerprint evidence. Fingerprints are marks formed by the contact of the little ridges on a person's fingers with some other substance. Latent prints are fingerprints that are formed from the oils on a person's hand. These are usually invisible to the naked eye. Investigators use powders that stick to these prints so that they can be seen more easily.

What makes fingerprints so useful is that the little ridges on a person's fingers are unique. Even identical twins have different fingerprints![8] Fingerprints are so useful that many people have made careers studying them.

fields of science. Physics can be used to find the path of a fallen drop of blood. Knowledge of chemistry can help identify a fiber. Biology can be used to identify the DNA in a drop of saliva. Every piece of evidence can help to catch a criminal, identify a victim, or reconstruct the events of a crime.

Early kinds of forensic science have been used since at least the eighth century. In the 700s, the Chinese used fingerprints to identify documents and sculptures. However, it was about a thousand years later that trace evidence began to develop as a way to solve crimes. In the eighteenth century, a man in England named John Toms was found guilty of murder in England because a piece of newspaper wadded in a pistol appeared to match a piece of paper found in his pocket. In 1835, Henry Goddard was working for Britain's Scotland Yard. He became the first to use analysis of a bullet to catch a murderer when he noticed a visible flaw in the bullet.[9]

Edmond Locard was the director of the first crime laboratory. Sometimes called "the Sherlock Holmes of France," Locard was an early forensic scientist and trace analyst. The basic idea of trace evidence is often known as "Locard's exchange principle," or "Locard's theory." It can be stated simply as: "Every contact leaves a trace."[10] His crime lab in Lyons, France, was an attic with two assistants to help him. However, it is partly because of his work that we now have specialists that work in many different fields of forensic science, such as fingerprints, bloodstain pattern analysis, DNA, and hair and fiber evidence.

Everyone leaves traces when they move from place to place. Suppose you go to a friend's house. You are wearing various items of clothing, all of which are made from different materials. Little bits of those materials, called fibers, may be caught on the furniture, or even blow off in the air. Not only that, but you may leave behind hairs, footprints, or even dirt from your shoes. Now suppose that a forensic scientist wants

When you go somewhere, you leave behind many traces—from your hair to your footprints.

TREE BARK

One type of clue that trace analysts study is tree bark. Tree bark can be found tracked inside from the outdoors, or even on a suspect. Tree bark is useful because there is a wide variety of bark on different trees. For instance, the bark of a pin oak tree is grayish-brown and usually thin and smooth. However, on a black oak, the bark is usually thick and very dark, with an orange inner bark. Bark works best as evidence when it comes from a tree that is uncommon in the area of the crime scene. If a suspect has a rare tree in his yard and bark from that kind of tree is found at a crime scene, the bark helps to link the suspect to the crime.

to prove that you were at your friend's house. Any piece of string or lint that comes off your clothes could be a useful clue. If those fibers are discovered and are compared to your clothes or fibers in your home, the forensic scientist would know that you were there.

Another common clue that criminals leave at a crime scene is hair. The average human being has about 5 million hairs, and those hairs are constantly falling out and being replaced. Anywhere you go, you may leave hairs behind—some of them so tiny that you can barely see them. Hair evidence can be used in several ways. Analyzing hair with a microscope can reveal important details about it, such as if it has ever been dyed or if it might have come from a certain kind of animal. Hair is also a source of DNA. DNA is the genetic material in living things— the molecules in a living thing's cells that tell the cells how to act. DNA is what makes a human a human or a cow a cow or a tree a tree.

If a forensic scientist looks at a hair under a microscope, he or she can make many observations that may help identify a victim or a suspect.

Everyone is different partly because almost everyone (except identical twins) has different DNA. Because everyone has different DNA, it is easy to identify who a hair belongs to. If a criminal leaves a hair at a crime scene, it is strong evidence that that person was at the scene.

Solving the Mystery of Mr. Fontaine

Detective Vidocq did not have the modern tools trace analysts do today. However, he was extremely careful to find and record the clues at the scene. And there were a lot of clues! Vidocq's investigation showed several types of trace evidence. He discovered footprints and made impressions of them to preserve them. He gathered up buttons found at the scene. He carefully picked up bits of paper, some of which were covered in blood. One clue was particularly important, though. Some of the bits of paper had writing on them.

Vidocq examined the writing. One bit said "Rao." He thought that this was probably the beginning of a name, perhaps "Raoul." Other bits seemed to be part of an address. By piecing together these clues, Vidocq came up with the name of a wine shop that the criminals may have visited. He sent some of his men in disguise to study the shop. They noticed two men, one of whom was named Raoul. One of them also had a limp, as if he had been recently injured. Because these people matched the evidence from the crime, Vidocq had the shop searched. They found even more trace evidence. The shop contained clothes that had been recently washed, but looked like they had blood on them. Finally, when the suspects were searched, one was found to have a wound that matched the victim's description.[11]

Vidocq believed he had discovered the attackers. He questioned them himself, and eventually the suspects confessed. Like Sherlock Holmes, Vidocq investigated every detail, even ones that did not seem important. Using those details—scraps of paper many people would

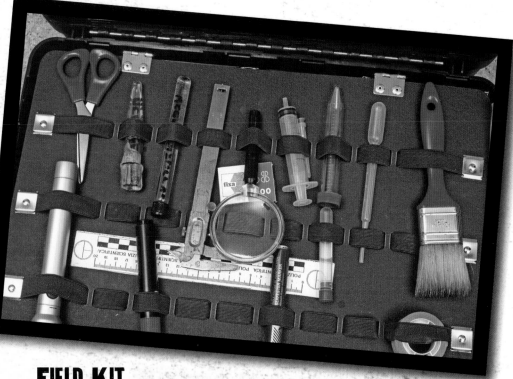

FIELD KIT

Forensic scientists who work at crime scenes use a lot of different tools. The set of tools a particular investigator uses at the crime scene is sometimes called a field kit. Common items in field kits include:

- tweezers, for picking up small objects
- paper, often specially made to avoid damaging evidence
- cotton swabs, to wipe things up
- razor blades, for cutting or scraping
- static lifts, which use static electricity to lift up evidence
- tape, including special tape for lifting evidence
- glass slides, for microscopes
- evidence vacuums, with filters
- lights, including special lights, such as UV
- envelopes, bags, or boxes, for storing gathered evidence
- markers or pens, to label the evidence bags

throw away as trash—he found his criminals and got their confessions. To this day, trace evidence deals with the little things not everyone notices. One crime scene processor said, "The key with trace evidence is, people aren't aware of it. A lot of times, it's not found. People at the scene might focus on other things."[12] Vidocq's capture of the men who attacked Fontaine was one of the first times trace evidence was used to catch a criminal, but it would not be the last.

Combing for Evidence

On July 17, 1982, Krista Harrison was collecting cans from a local baseball park in Ohio with a friend named Roy. According to Roy, a dark van drove into the park and a man got out. He approached Harrison and spoke to her briefly. Then the two of them got into the van and drove away together.

Several days later, on July 23, Harrison's body was found. She had been strangled. Police also found a second crime scene. While Harrison's body had been left in one location, the murder had probably been committed in another. The second crime scene had other clues. They included a garbage bag, some cardboard, and a blanket. Some of these items had blood and hair on them. Police also examined the place where Harrison's body had been found and discovered a pair of jeans and a plaid shirt. The jeans had specks of blood and paint on them. There was a lot of evidence to go through, but the investigators were careful to examine each piece. They even noticed some tiny fibers on Harrison's body—fibers that might lead them to her killer. [1]

Evidence must be examined carefully for any traces of hair, fiber, blood, or other substances that might lead to a suspect.

Fiber Evidence

Fiber evidence is a common kind of trace evidence. A fiber is a small, long piece of material. Fibers are sometimes woven together to make strings or fabrics. Many things we see or use every day are made of fibers, including clothes, carpets, plants, paper, and even paper money. Because we use fibers all the time, they sometimes stick to our bodies or our clothes. We can move them as we go from place to place. Suppose a boy went to visit his aunt and when he arrived she gave him a hug. A fiber from her sweater might rub off on the boy's t-shirt. If someone were to find the fiber and recognize where it came from, they would have evidence that the boy had been with his aunt. Evidence is the name we give to objects and facts that help us prove something is true. Because the boy had a fiber from his aunt's sweater on his t-shirt, it is probably true that he was with her.

Fiber evidence is usually examined by fiber analysts. They use a variety of techniques to collect any tiny evidence that may be available. Sometimes a piece of torn fabric can simply be picked up and matched to another piece. Other times, a fiber analyst will use tweezers to pick up smaller evidence. They may even literally comb a victim's hair looking for fibers. No tool for collecting fibers is perfect. Some fiber analysts use regular household tape or specialized lifting tape to pick up tiny particles of fiber for later examination, but this is not always a good idea. The sticky tape can **contaminate** the evidence. Another tool is a static lift. A static lift is made of plastic and uses static electricity to pick up fibers. Static electricity is an electric charge that develops naturally on certain objects and can sometimes make them stick to one another. Small fibers will stick to the static lift without being contaminated by any sticky substance. However, static electricity can cause electric sparks. These sparks can destroy evidence, or even damage equipment.[2]

CORDAGE

Cordage is a general term for rope, string, and other things that are made of long fibers twisted together. Cordage can be examined and grouped by a number of different traits. The following traits help identify the fibers and match them to a crime scene, suspect, or victim:

• diameter, or width

• if and how the fibers are twisted together

• the number of fibers in each string

• the number of times the cord is twisted per inch of cord

• the direction of the twist in the cord

• if the strings in the fiber have a core

• the type of fibers used in the cord

What Type of Fiber?

Once fibers have been collected, investigators work to identify the fiber. What makes fiber evidence so useful is that there are many different types of fibers. If a match can be found between two different fibers, it can be strong evidence that they are from the same place. According to one fiber specialist, "Every year, worldwide, there's somewhere around one hundred *billion* pounds of fiber produced. *Every year*. And think about this: When you're in a large department store, or on public transit, or in an airport—any place where there's a lot of people—how often do you find two people wearing exactly the same garment? . . . The variety in textiles is *enormous*. Variety is our friend in forensic science."[3]

The huge variety of fibers means that fiber analysts need different ways to classify fibers. Some fibers are natural; they came from a plant, animal, or mineral. Cotton is the most common plant fiber used to make fabrics. The most common animal fiber used in fabrics is wool.[4] Less common natural fibers may be more useful to forensic scientists—as a rule, the less common a fiber is, the better evidence it is. Less common natural fibers include flax (or linen), cashmere, alpaca, and many others. Other fibers are **synthetic**, or man-made, such as polyester or nylon. Synthetic fibers are often easy to tell from natural fibers because synthetic fibers usually begin as a liquid and are squeezed through a nozzle to form strands. Some synthetic fibers have cross-sections with unusual or unique shapes. A cross-section of an object is what that object would look like if you took a slice from the middle of it. The cross-section of a strand of spaghetti would look like a small circle. On the other hand, a cross-section of a strand of fettuccine would look like a flat rectangle. You can tell many fibers apart in the same way. The fiber's shape under a microscope can identify it as natural or synthetic, what kind of material it is, and who created it. Some fibers have shapes that are only used by certain manufacturers, while others are simple shapes that are very common.

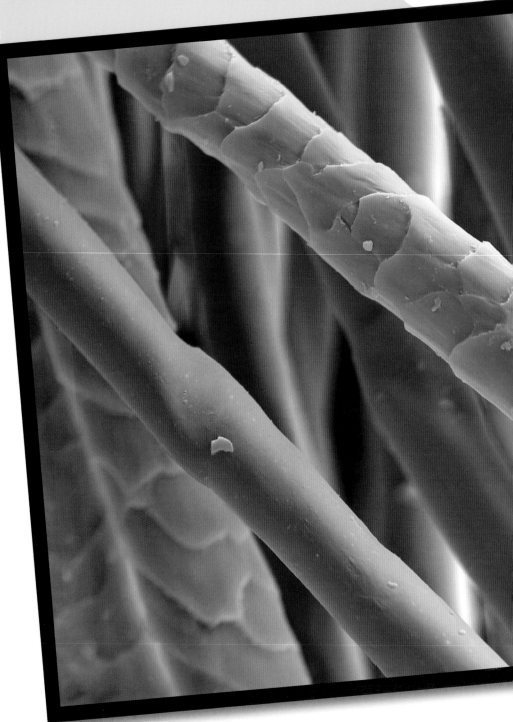

This image is magnified 1,000 times. The white fibers are wool (natural) and the orange fibers are synthetic. Can you spot the difference?

This is useful for a forensic scientist, because if a fiber's shape is uncommon, that means that there are very few places that fiber could have come from.

Investigators may also examine a fiber's color. Color analysis, or **spectrophotometry**, is not as simple as whether a fabric is red or blue, or dark or light—it includes every way that a substance interacts with light.

To understand spectrophotometry, you must first understand that white light is actually made up of many different colors of light all mixed together. All these colors of light form the visible spectrum—all the colors humans can see. If you look closely at a television or a computer monitor, you may find that what appears to be white is actually made up of tiny bits of red, blue, and green light mixed together. This is the reason that we sometimes see rainbows after a storm—tiny droplets of water in the air separate the sunlight into its different parts so we can see them. This separation of white light into colored light is how we get all the colors we see in white light. The reason that an apple appears red is that when white light hits it, the red part of the light is separated from the rest and bounces off so we can see it. Using spectrophotometers, scientists can identify objects much more accurately than just by using their eyes.[5]

While the color itself is important in identifying a fiber, forensic scientists can also tell how the fiber was colored. Just because two fibers are both red does not mean they come from the same place. One may have been dyed when it was made—its color may be part of the fiber itself. Another may have been dyed after being used in a fabric, so that the dye is on top of the original color of the fiber. Other fibers get their color from having been printed on, like a t-shirt with words or a design. This printing process can have differences as well—one fiber may have been printed on with ink while another may have been printed on with paint. If the color of a fiber has faded or discolored, that may also link it to an item that has similar fading and discoloration.[6]

LIGHTING

The visible spectrum is a small part of all light. While humans can only see this type of light, spectrophotometers may be able to sense much more. Fibers that may react the same way to the visible spectrum of light may also react differently to infrared (light that has lower energy than red light) and ultraviolet (light that has higher energy than violet light). Some fibers might even glow in ultraviolet light! Trace analysts will often use several different light sources to find and identify evidence.

Rare Fibers

The fibers that investigators noticed on Krista Harrison's body were unusual. They were synthetic fibers with an orange color, and a trilobal shape—meaning that the cross-section of the fiber had three parts, a little like the letter Y. The trilobal shape of these fibers was unusual. Not many manufacturers of synthetic fibers used this particular shape. Investigators knew that if they could find similar fibers in a suspect's home or car it would be good evidence that Harrison had been with that suspect. The rare fibers would make it seem very unlikely that Harrison had gotten the fibers anywhere else.

Of course, first the police had to find a suspect. To narrow their search, they first focused on the plastic that had been found wrapped around the body. The plastic, along with other evidence, was sent to Ohio's Bureau of Criminal Identification and Investigation (BCI). BCI determined that the plastic was a bag that had once contained seats for a van. Specifically, they were seats ordered at a Sears department store. The detectives contacted Sears for further information. The department store provided the investigators with a list of people in the area who had ordered the seats, but unfortunately this was a very long list. The detectives researched and interviewed everyone whose name was on the list, but they could not determine who the killer was without more information.

Two months later, a break came in the case. A twenty-eight-year-old woman had escaped after being kidnapped and tortured by a man named Robert Buell. Buell was caught and pled no contest to the charges against him, meaning that he refused to either admit to or deny the charges. He was sentenced to 121 years in prison. However, investigators thought Buell might be guilty of other crimes, too. They recognized his name from the list Sears had provided. Could Buell also be the killer of Krista Harrison?

Police obtained **search warrants** and searched Buell's home. They discovered a variety of evidence, including clothing, dog hairs, candles, and a roll of orange carpet. The carpet had been used in a van like the one Harrison's friend had seen her get into—and the van contained new seats from Sears. When the carpet was examined, investigators discovered that the fibers in it were synthetic and orange. Not only that, but it was made from trilobal fibers that appeared to be the same as those that had been found on Harrison's body. It now seemed very likely that Buell was the killer. Martin Frantz was the assistant prosecutor during Buell's trial, meaning that he was a lawyer whose job it was to prove that Buell was guilty. He said, " . . . we had someone figure out, mathematically, how many people in the world could possibly be connected to all of that circumstantial evidence that we found inside Buell's home. It was something like 1 in 6 trillion."

Buell was put on trial for Krista Harrison's murder. Because of the overwhelming evidence, a jury found him guilty.[7]

Not Quite Spotless

When investigating a suspect, one of the first places any trace analyst will check is in the suspect's car. "Cars are a great source of evidence," says one trace analyst. "There are layers of trace in a car. The inside of it is like a bucket. You come into it, you move around. You're depositing trace evidence. You leave, you come back the next day, you add more, you add more. There's a *wealth* of trace on the inside of the vehicle."[1] It's easy to see why a suspect's vehicle is so useful to investigators. Sometimes vehicles transport a criminal to and from a crime. Other times vehicles are the locations of crimes, including kidnapping. Other times, a criminal's vehicle isn't just a tool—it's actually a weapon.

On January 24, 2001, Erik Schrieffer disappeared. Schrieffer was a motorcycle enthusiast, or "biker", who had been staying at a bar called the Hog Pen. Bikers suddenly disappearing wasn't that unusual, as many of them traveled around. When Schrieffer went missing, police investigated, but they didn't expect to have much success. Weeks passed, and the case was rapidly growing cold. The police had found nothing until two witnesses came forward.

The witnesses were bikers, just like Schrieffer. They told police that they had seen Schrieffer get into an argument with another biker named Joseph Wehmanen on the night of his disappearance. The argument, they said, had ended in murder.

According to the witnesses, the two men had gotten into a fistfight in the bar that spilled out into the road. Wehmanen won the fight, and left Schrieffer hurt in the street. Going to his truck, Wehmanen didn't just drive away. Instead, he ran straight over Schrieffer. After this act of violence, the witnesses claimed Wehmanen grabbed Schrieffer and threw him in the back of the truck. [2]

Hit and Run

The easiest way to track down a vehicle involved in a crime is with an eyewitness. The witness can provide a variety of information. The information may be as

This forensic scientist is collecting paint evidence from the bumper of a car.

MAKING AN IMPRESSION

When a car hits a person, obviously the car leaves its mark on the victim. However, a victim may also leave a mark on the car.

When a victim of a car accident slides across the paint of a car, it produces heat. This heat can soften the paint on the car. The soft paint can then stick to the fibers in the victim's clothing. If a trace analyst examines these fibers, he or she can use them to link the car to the victim's clothing.

Sometimes, people can leave even more of a mark. In Connie Fletcher's *Every Contact Leaves a Trace*, one crime lab director repeated a story told by forensic scientist Henry Lee. "A state trooper was assisting a motorist and got hit by a truck and killed. When they finally found the truck . . . the front edge of the trailer has an imprint of the Connecticut State Police patch that was on the guy's right shoulder."[4] That kind of evidence is going to be difficult to explain as a coincidence!

simple as the color and kind of vehicle, but a really good eyewitness report can tell you the make and model of the car, or the license plate number. However, trace specialists have a number of other ways to link a car to a crime.

One of those ways is to use paint. Remember that every contact leaves a trace. With a powerful contact like a car accident, there will often be unusual traces. You might not expect clothes to be strong enough to take paint off a vehicle. However, when a car hits a victim, the force of the car can smash some of the paint into the victim's clothes. A trace analyst might be able to get some of that paint from the clothes and use it to run tests. If the car has its original paint, the kind of paint on the clothing can indicate what kind of car hit the victim. In the words of one trace analyst, ". . . with a victim that was hit by a vehicle, we'll take his or her clothing and scrape it and look for paint. We have a database called PDQ, Paint Data Query . . . If we find paint on a victim, we can run it through the database and possibly get a make and model of the vehicle."[3]

Another source of trace evidence from cars is tire tracks. Tire tracks are more complicated than you might think. To get the most out of a tire track, an analyst must be able to understand many things about how tracks are made and how they go together. Tire tracks can tell an investigator whether a vehicle was a car or truck or how big and heavy the vehicle was. The pattern of the track tread can help an investigator figure out what kind of tire made the track. Some tires are only available on certain vehicles, so a tire track can reveal what kind of car or truck the criminal was driving.

Tires wear down over time. Any two tires rarely wear down in exactly the same way, though. This means that even tires that were the same when they were new might be very different a year later. Analysts can sometimes identify not only the type of car a criminal used, but the car itself based on the tire tracks.[5]

After the witnesses came forward in the case of Erik Schrieffer, investigators went to the scene of the alleged crime. It had snowed several times since the incident, but the investigators managed to find evidence—blood. They dug through the snow to find as much of the blood as they could and collected it. There was a lot of blood in the snow—so much that they could presume that Schrieffer had been murdered.

The eyewitness reports had now been backed up by evidence at the scene. The police arrested Wehmanen for murder. However, their witnesses had disappeared, and there was no tire track evidence to be found. They also still had not found Schrieffer's body. The police would need more evidence to convince a jury that Wehmanen was guilty.

FOOTPRINTS

Human footprints are similar to tire tracks in many ways. Footprints can give clues to the height and weight of the person who made them. The treads of someone's shoes may have a pattern unique to that brand or type of shoe. And like tires, shoes wear down in different ways over time. Because footprints are so useful and so complex, some trace analysts specialize in studying them. One footwear impression specialist said, "Take your shoes off and look at the bottom of your shoes. What you'll see, in addition to the general wear patterns, are a whole bunch of unique, random marks, scratches, gouges . . . I can take a police department with five hundred police officers that all wear the same boot, and we can differentiate each pair from all the others."[6]

Tire tracks can tell a crime scene investigator (CSI) many things about a vehicle, including how heavy it was and whether it was a car or a truck.

The obvious place to look for evidence was the suspected murder weapon—Wehmanen's truck.

The truck was taken to a lab to be examined. The analysts worked on the truck for three months. After all that time, what the analysts found was . . . nothing. There was no trace of hairs or fibers from the victim. They found no blood, no skin, and no fingerprints that could have come

These CSIs are examining tire tracks to help find potential suspects in an arson case.

from the victim. The police thought they had the right suspect, but somehow the truck seemed to be spotless!

The police were right. Joseph Wehmanen had killed Erik Schrieffer. Unfortunately, he had used a pressure washer to clean up his truck. A pressure washer is a machine that uses powerful sprays of water to clean surfaces very well. The water jets are so strong that they can be very dangerous and should never be directed at people or animals. The pressure washer Wehmanen used to try and hide his crime almost made it impossible for police to convict him.

However, the investigators were not going to give up easily. After they got the truck back from the lab, they decided to examine it themselves. At first, they had no more luck than the lab did. They looked over every inch of the truck. They searched the inside and the outside. They examined underneath the car and they looked at the roof.

Finally, they found it: a trace of blood. Some blood had been splashed up into the top of the truck, hidden behind part of the frame. This could be just the evidence they needed to prove Wehmanen was guilty.[7]

A Confession of Sorts

When prosecutors revealed that they had found blood in Wehmanen's car, Wehmanen immediately decided to plead guilty to murder. Wehmanen confessed to running over Schrieffer, but he told a story that did not match the reports of the witnesses and was very difficult to believe.

According to Wehmanen, Erik Schrieffer had threatened him with a gun. Another biker had taken the gun and offered it to Wehmanen. Wehmanen had refused to shoot Schrieffer, though. He had simply driven off. However, while driving away he accidentally hit Schrieffer with his car. Wehmanen had tried to help Schrieffer by driving him to the hospital.

That was where Wehmanen's supposed good behavior ended, though. Wehmanen decided he couldn't take Schrieffer to the hospital because it would look like he was a murderer. Instead, he made sure Schrieffer was dead and robbed him. Then he took the body to a frozen river and drilled a hole in the ice. He dumped the body in the river and cleaned out his truck.

Because police had not discovered a body and had relatively little evidence, Wehmanen did not get punished as harshly as many people thought he deserved. He was sentenced to eight years in prison. However, we can all be grateful that investigators worked so hard to find the evidence that proved Wehmanen guilty. Without a trace of blood found in the killer's car, Wehmanen would probably have never been brought to justice.[8]

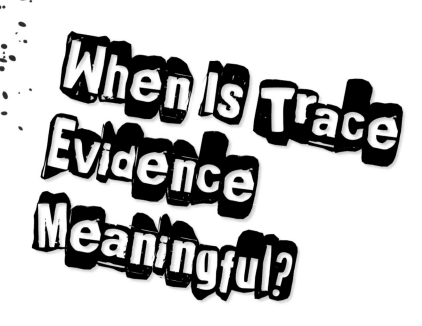

When Is Trace Evidence Meaningful?

n the case of Erik Schrieffer, an eyewitness account led the investigators to trace evidence. That trace evidence helped the police get a confession from the suspect. However, how useful would the trace evidence have been on its own? It is important to remember that trace evidence is a form of **circumstantial evidence**. Circumstantial evidence is evidence that is indirect. If a murder is caught on videotape, it can be used as direct evidence that a suspect committed the crime. However, suppose a victim's body has a fiber on it and that fiber is found at a suspect's home. The fiber does not directly show that the suspect murdered the victim, like a videotape of the crime would. It only directly shows that the victim was in the suspect's home. That fact is what makes it seem likely the suspect is the murderer.

Circumstantial evidence is weaker than direct evidence. Investigators and juries have to decide if trace evidence is meaningful. If a victim's body is found with blue threads from denim jeans and a suspect owns denim jeans, then that may not be useful evidence. Many people own denim jeans and blue is a very popular color for them, so the link to the suspect is very weak. How do we know when trace evidence is good evidence and when it is not?

This was the question presented to juries during the trial of Wayne Williams.

A series of murders and disappearances occurred in Atlanta, Georgia, from 1979 to 1981.[1] Many people thought that the crimes were all linked due to similarities between the victims and similar kinds of evidence being found at several different crime scenes. Over the course of two years, at least twenty-nine people are believed to have been victims of a serial killer, a murderer who kills many people over thirty days or more.

LINKING CRIMES

When a number of disappearances or murders occur in the same area, it is natural to suppose they might be linked. But in a large city there may be several murders that are unrelated in a short period of time. How can we know when different crimes are actually the work of one criminal?

In the case of the murders in Atlanta, there were two reasons: similar evidence and similar victims. Fibers found on some of the victims appeared to be from the same source, and the victims were all African-Americans. Because the crimes were so similar, people thought they were connected— but these are educated guesses, not solid facts.

Another way crimes can be similar is called a **modus operandi**, or MO. An MO is the particular way a crime is committed. To a forensic investigator, the way a crime is committed can be good evidence that the crimes are all connected.

The hunt for the killer became a national news sensation, and lasted for many months. The man eventually convicted of two of these deaths, and blamed for the others, was Wayne Williams.

Suppose for a moment that you are a member of a jury in a trial. It is your responsibility to decide if the defendant, the person on trial, has been proven guilty by the prosecutor, the lawyer presenting the case against the defendant. The prosecutor attempts to prove to you that the defendant is guilty, and the defendant's lawyer or lawyers try to show that the defendant is not. In the United States, a defendant is considered innocent until he or she is proven guilty beyond a reasonable doubt. This means that if you, on the jury, think there's a reasonable possibility that the defendant is innocent, you should find him or her not guilty. This idea of reasonable doubt is key to many suspected criminals' defenses.

In the trial of Wayne Williams, the prosecution presented the jury with many pieces of evidence. One was the report of police officers who had been on a stakeout at the James Jackson Parkway Bridge in May of 1981. After nearly two years of murders and disappearances, the police and the FBI were both working hard to catch the killer. The police had been watching the bridge because a number of bodies had been found there. One police officer on duty, Officer Bob Campbell, heard the sounds of something splashing into the water and a car driving over the bridge. The other officer on the stakeout, Officer Freddie Jacobs, saw the car and identified it as a 1970 Chevrolet station wagon. A third officer stationed nearby, Officer Carl Holden, noticed the car and had it followed. The car was eventually pulled over by FBI Agent Greg Gilliland.[2]

The driver of the car was Wayne Williams. As a music promoter, he claimed that he was on his way to meet a potential client named Cheryl Johnson. However, the phone number he provided for this client was incorrect and he claimed he had been driving to a place that did not exist.

Do you know who's who in this courtroom scene?
The judge is at the top left, and the twelve jury members are to the right.

Williams's vehicle was searched and he was questioned for over an hour. The river beneath the lake was searched, but police found no trace of a body. The next day, police questioned Williams again. Then, a day later, the body of Nathaniel Cater was found in the river near where Officer Campbell had heard a splash. It appeared that Cater had been dead for a few days—just long enough that it was possible Williams had thrown his body off the bridge.

This testimony was not convincing evidence of a crime by itself. The prosecutor's evidence did not end there. Many fibers had been found on the victims the police had discovered. Williams's home was searched, and many samples of fibers were taken to be analyzed. The FBI laboratories took these various fibers and analyzed them. Among the fibers they took were a number of hairs.

Hair Evidence

Hair is a kind of fiber found only on mammals. Hairs from different mammals may have different qualities, but all types of hair have some similarities.[3]

All hairs are mostly made of keratin, the same substance that makes up human fingernails. Hairs have three main regions—the **cuticle**, the **cortex**, and the **medulla**. The cuticle is a thin, scaly covering of the outside of the hair. The shape of the scales in the cuticle is one of the ways to identify the kind of hair you're looking at. The cortex is the main body of a hair. The cortex may contain little spaces of air as well as bits of color. The medulla is the central core of the hair. Not all hairs have a visible medulla, and in some hairs the medulla is filled with air. The structure of the cells in the medulla is another good way to distinguish between different types of hairs, particularly between humans and different types of animals.

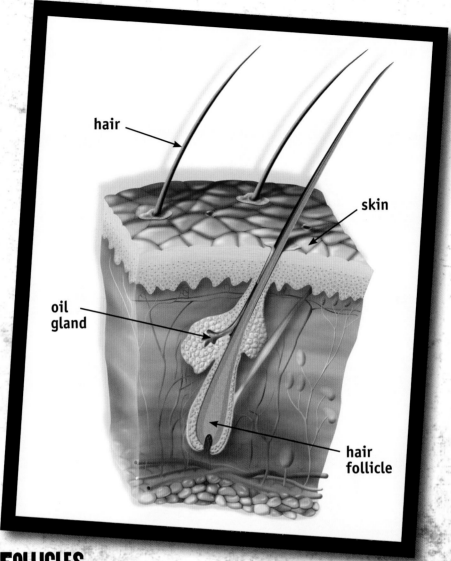

hair

skin

oil
gland

hair
follicle

FOLLICLES

Hairs in mammals grow out of tiny sockets in the skin called follicles. Follicles are groups of cells that grow into a cup-like shape. The follicle is mostly below the skin, but it also pokes out of the skin slightly. The hair grows up and out of the follicle. The base of the follicle contains the cells that make the hair grow. When the hair stops growing, it rests in the follicle for some time before being lost. However, when a hair is plucked out it may take some of the follicle, or even the surrounding skin, with it. These hairs can provide good material for forensic testing.

This instrument is used to find traces of drugs and other chemicals in human hair.

While a lot of trace hair evidence is human, animal hair can be useful as well. Animal hairs found at crime scenes can help show that a suspect who has a pet was at the scene. There are a number of ways to tell human hair from animal hair. Human hair is usually of a consistent color, while animal hairs may look like they are striped. The medulla in a human hair usually has no pattern to it, while in an animal hair it may have any one of a number of patterns. The color in human hairs is usually consistent throughout the structure of a hair or focused on the cuticle, while in an animal hair the color is usually focused around the medulla. Human hairs can also be identified by the size and shape of the hair's root.

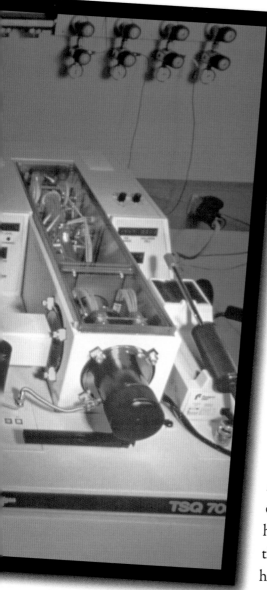

It is not usually possible to tell many distinguishing characteristics about people from their hair. A hair can give clues to its owner's ethnicity, but gender and age are harder to determine. Because of this, hair analysts do not usually use hair evidence alone. Instead, they compare the hair evidence to hairs taken from suspects or victims and see if the hairs are similar. Usually the shape of the hair under a microscope is used to link a hair to a suspect, but sometimes an analyst can use other methods. Because hair grows from your body, hair sometimes picks up chemicals in your body, such as medicine or illegal drugs. If a chemical analysis of a hair reveals a certain type of drug, and a suspect is known to have used that drug, that is more evidence that the hair came from that suspect.

Using microscopes and chemical tests to analyze hair, a hair analyst can usually say one of three things:

- The hair evidence is similar to hairs from the suspect or victim and may have come from the same source.

- The hair evidence is different from the hairs of the suspect or victim and did not come from the same source.

- The hairs do not contain enough information to allow them to come to a meaningful conclusion.

These results can be used to identify a victim when no other means of identification are available, or tie an object to a victim to determine if it was used as a murder weapon. And, of course, they can point police toward a possible killer.

Convicted by a Hair

In the case of Wayne Williams, the hairs that were used against him were not his own, but his dog's. Dog hair found at the scene of some of the murders was compared to hair that investigators had taken from Williams's dog. The hairs were alike. Suppose you are a juror in the trial. The prosecutor tells you that over twenty-eight fibers, including dog hair, that were found on the victims' bodies have been matched to fibers found in Wayne Williams's home and car. Fiber analysts say that it is likely the victims picked up the fibers in Williams's home. The prosecution even claims that there are so many matches between the victims and Williams that it is statistically impossible for the victims to not have been in Williams's home and car. Do you think you would find Williams guilty based on this kind of evidence?

In January of 1982, a jury did find Williams guilty of two murders.[4] However, Williams's attorneys decided to appeal the conviction. These attorneys argued that there were many potential problems with the fiber evidence used by the prosecutor. While many fibers were found on the various victims, some people thought the prosecutor had not really proven that all the murders were related. What if the victims had been

WOOL

Wool is a specialized type of animal hair. Wool is found on sheep, goats, llamas, and even some rabbits. Wool is more useful than most other animal hairs because of its length and the crimped shape of its fibers. This shape allows it to be bound together and woven into fabrics. Because of this, wool is commonly used in clothing and other materials. This means that even though wool is a hair, it is often treated more like other fibers in analysis—it is unusual for a criminal to have a pet sheep!

Wayne Williams was convicted of murder based on hair evidence from his dog.

killed by different people? Then it would not make any sense to use evidence from all the victims together to convict Williams. Further, most of the fibers used in evidence were actually very common. The prosecutors had presented their fiber evidence as if it were conclusive fact, when the evidence might have been coincidental. In fact, one of the prosecutor's key pieces of evidence was a fiber found on the body of a man named Clifford Jones. Because of that fiber, they believed Jones had been in proximity to Wayne Williams's home. However, Jones had been killed in the back of a Laundromat, where hundreds of fibers can be found all over the place. They argued that no fiber could be really meaningful when it may have come from someone's laundry instead of the killer. Finally, while many fibers that matched Williams's home and car were found on various victims, no fibers from the victims were ever found in Williams's home or car. How could he have left traces on the victims without the victims ever leaving traces on him?

With this new information, do you think there would be a reasonable doubt that Williams was actually guilty? Chet Dettlinger, who had investigated the murders before Williams was arrested, was not convinced that the true culprit had been caught. "I don't know if Wayne Williams is innocent or not," he once said. "'I just don't think they proved him guilty of anything."[5]

Wayne Williams's appeals were rejected, and he is still in prison today. We may never know with certainty if Williams is innocent or guilty. Many people still debate whether hair and fiber evidence alone is convincing enough to convict a suspect, but trace evidence can provide powerful support for other evidence or provide important leads.

5

Piling on the Evidence

n the case of Wayne Williams, the prosecutor presented dozens of hairs and fibers and many people were still unconvinced. So when is trace evidence good enough to overcome reasonable doubt?

Trace evidence is circumstantial evidence. One of the ways circumstantial evidence is useful is in supporting other evidence. Suppose there is a break-in at a jewelry store and a security guard identifies a suspect. A jury might not want to take the guard's word, in case he happened to be mistaken. However, if there is circumstantial evidence at the scene—like fibers or fingerprints—that supports the security guard's story, a jury may be more likely to believe the security guard.

The other way for circumstantial evidence to be useful is for there to be a lot of it, with many sources effectively supporting each other. If several types of evidence are all found pointing to a suspect, it becomes very unlikely that the suspect is not involved in the crime.

A Missing Girl

Danielle van Dam went to sleep at her home on February 1, 2002.[1] The next morning, she was nowhere to be found. Her parents immediately called the police. Police searched about two hundred houses nearby, but found no trace of van Dam. Someone else was missing as well, though. David Westerfield, a neighbor of the Van Dams, was not home when the police knocked on his door. Later, he claimed he had been on a two-day trip around the country in a mobile home he owned. The police were suspicious of him—it seemed like a strange coincidence that he had disappeared just as van Dam had.

Van Dam's disappearance became a national news story. Volunteers from all over the country came to help search for the missing girl. After weeks of investigating, police still thought Westerfield might be involved. This suspicion seemed to be confirmed when police discovered an important piece of circumstantial evidence. Westerfield brought a number of linens and a jacket to the dry cleaners. After taking the jacket as evidence, police discovered that it was contaminated with van Dam's blood. With this powerful evidence behind them, the police believed that they could prove that Westerfield had kidnapped the girl, and they arrested him. Just a few days later, her body was found. The police were now investigating a murder and they had already arrested the most likely suspect.

Now that they had evidence against Westerfield, they could go and look for more. Investigators searched Westerfield's home and the mobile home in which he had traveled. They discovered a variety of trace evidence. They took a number of hairs, both animal and human, as well as fibers and more blood. Some of the human hairs found matched van Dam's hair, while some animal hairs matched the hair of the van Dams' dog. Further, there were fibers matching the van Dam's carpet. Blood and hair found in the mobile home were tested for DNA.

David Westerfield's jacket is held up as evidence during court proceedings.

DNA Evidence

DNA (deoxyribonucleic acid) is a kind of blueprint for your body. All living things have DNA, and almost everyone's DNA is different. DNA can be found in most of the cells in your body, including white blood cells and hair cells. Scientists can perform tests that match DNA evidence to a suspect or victim with a high degree of probability.

DNA is extremely useful to trace analysts because many kinds of traces contain DNA. Hairs can be analyzed for DNA. Traces of blood contain DNA. Other bodily fluids, such as saliva, also contain it. Objects that have been in someone's mouth might even have enough saliva on them to produce results. One way or the other, an investigator probably would not have trouble finding your DNA anywhere you spend a lot of time, like school or work.

DNA contains four different amino acids: cytosine (C), thymine (T), adenine (A), and guanine (G). How could only four amino acids write out the directions to make an entire human being? The answer is that although DNA is very tiny, it contains billions of these amino acids. Think of the amino acids like digits in a number. We only use ten digits (zero through nine), but those ten digits can be combined to write any number.

In order to identify a person by his or her DNA, scientists use extremely precise techniques of DNA analysis. They do this by examining very small sections of DNA and looking at the ACTGs. With modern DNA analysis, a scientist can often determine with very high certainty that a DNA sample came from a specific person.[2]

DNA analysis is one of many sciences that trace analysts use to find clues about crimes. "DNA and trace can often work together," said one trace analyst. "DNA can answer the important question, 'Was the guy here?' Trace can answer the question, 'What was his intent? What did he do?'"[3]

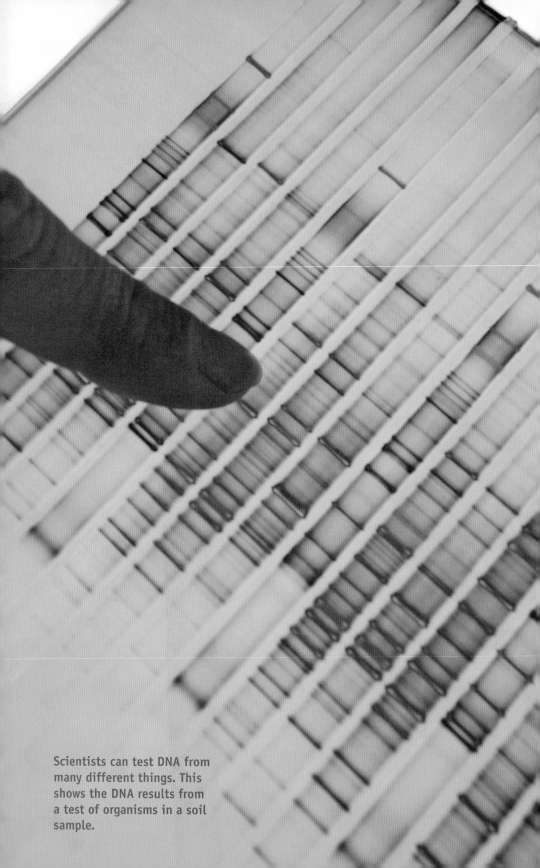

Scientists can test DNA from many different things. This shows the DNA results from a test of organisms in a soil sample.

These sciences working together does not stop a little friendly competition, of course. Some trace experts like to put it this way: A DNA specialist only has to worry about one little molecule—a trace analyst has to worry about all of them![4]

Beyond a Reasonable Doubt

In the case of Danielle van Dam, one expert claimed that, based on the DNA evidence, there was only a one in 670 quadrillion chance that the blood police had found on Westerfield's jacket could belong to someone other than Danielle van Dam.[5] A quadrillion is equal to a million multiplied by a million multiplied by a thousand! That means that you would probably need about a hundred million times the people on the entire planet Earth to find another match.

However, no matter how precise it is, even DNA evidence is circumstantial. The police had proven that van Dam's blood was on Westerfield's jacket, but they could not prove for certain how it

HOW MUCH INFORMATION IS IN A CELL?

As you know, DNA contains billions of amino acids. Yet DNA fits inside cells that are so tiny they cannot be seen without a microscope. Your DNA is curled up tight in the cells of your body. In fact, they are curled so tight that if you stretched out all the DNA from one of your cells, it would probably be taller than you are!

Each DNA molecule is amazingly small, but altogether they contain a huge amount of information. In fact, if the genetic information located in a single human DNA molecule was written out, it would fill about one hundred twenty-five Manhattan telephone books. You have billions of DNA molecules in your body, so imagine how big the book with all your information in it would be!

had gotten there. The amount of blood was small enough that even a nosebleed could have been responsible. The police needed more evidence to make sure Westerfield was convicted.

The hairs and fibers found in Westerfield's mobile home could be used to back up the blood evidence. Trace evidence analyst Tanya Dulaney was called upon to explain some of the evidence during the trial. "I observed one human hair that was similar to Danielle's," she said, referring to a blond hair found in Westerfield's home.[6] Further, a number

CELL STRUCTURE— DNA IN THE NUCLEUS

Human cells are made up of many different parts. They are contained within a cellular membrane, which is kind of like the skin of the cell. Inside the cell are a variety of organelles, small structures that do different jobs to keep the cell alive. Most of the DNA of a cell rests in the cell's nucleus, which is like the brain of the cell. Only cells that have a nucleus can usually be used for DNA analysis. This means that even though blood is one of the best sources of DNA, red blood cells do not actually contain any! It is white blood cells that provide the DNA used in forensic tests.

of hairs were found that could have been from the van Dam's dog, as well as microscopic fibers that matched those found in the van Dam's carpet. This evidence made it likely that not only had Westerfield been around van Dam, but he had been inside the van Dam home. One of van Dam's fingerprints was also found on a cabinet inside Westerfield's motor home. The evidence clearly indicated van Dam had been inside his home. "Danielle van Dam touched that cabinet," said fingerprint analyst Jeffrey Graham.[7]

Perhaps Westerfield could have explained why van Dam's blood was on his jacket, but could he explain why her hair, fingerprints, and blood were also in his home? And why he had

FORENSIC ENTOMOLOGY

There is one type of small clue that forensic scientists sometimes deal with that is not usually considered trace evidence—insects. The study of insects is called entomology. David Westerfield's defense lawyers had experts who believed that they could prove Westerfield innocent with entomology. When a body is left outside, it quickly attracts insects. Those insects feed on the body and lay eggs in it. If an investigator knows enough about the insects in the body, he or she can estimate how long a victim has been dead. Some scientists who examined van Dam's body believed that she had actually been killed after Westerfield was being watched by the police. There did not seem to be enough insects on her body for her to have been dead very long. However, other experts disagreed, and the defense's arguments did not convince the jury.

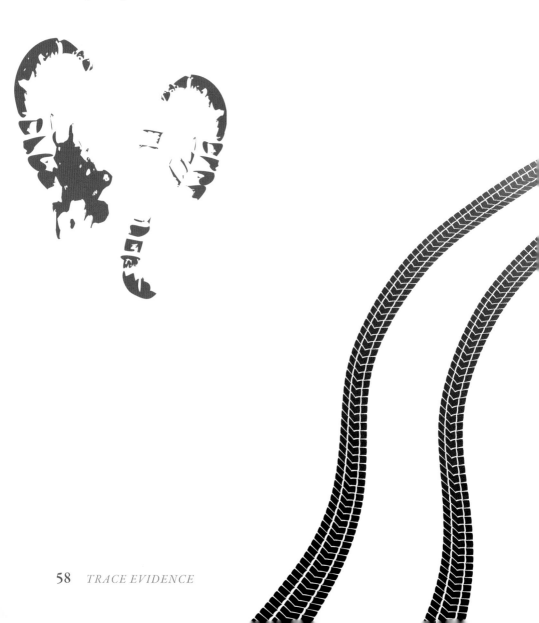

been in her bedroom? "No explanation except for guilt. None," said prosecutor Jeff Dusek.[8]

Westerfield's trial lasted three months. In August of 2002, a jury found him guilty of kidnapping and murder. Because of trace evidence and DNA science, van Dam's family can be sure that her killer was brought to justice.[9]

Vanished With a Trace

We know that trace evidence can link a suspect to the location of a body, or a body to a suspect's home or vehicle. But what about when there is no body to compare the evidence to? Yes, it is still possible to catch a killer without a body or a confession. Sometimes the combined weight of trace evidence is so strong that prosecutors can achieve a conviction for murder even when the body of the victim has never been found. And sometimes that evidence is as simple as a roll of duct tape.

In 1991, Scott Dunn was a young man living in Lubbock, Texas. He worked installing stereo systems in cars, and he had a passion for it. According to his father, James, "He got into the thing he liked the most. These loud, high-powered car stereos. They seemed to be his life."[1] His love for loud music had even earned him a nickname: his friends called him "Iceman" because he tried to use ice to make speakers play louder. He had even taken the back seats out of his car so he could put bigger speakers in. Because Dunn had a job working with the cars and stereo equipment that he loved, it was very unusual when he failed to show up for work one day.

In May of that year, Dunn called in sick to work for two days. This was not unusual, and after this absence, he let a co-worker know that he was going to come back to work. However, when the co-worker stopped by Dunn's apartment the next day, no one answered the door. Dunn did not show up to work, and the police were soon contacted. No one has seen Scott Dunn since.[2]

How does one prove a murder has occurred when the victim's body has not been found? One way is to start with blood. Police Detective Tal English spoke to Dunn's roommate and ex-girlfriend, Leisha Hamilton. Hamilton told Detective English that a piece of carpet was missing from their apartment. "Well, if there was a piece of missing carpet, there was a reason for it, and I wondered what was on it," Detective English later said.[3] When he and Detective George White investigated Dunn

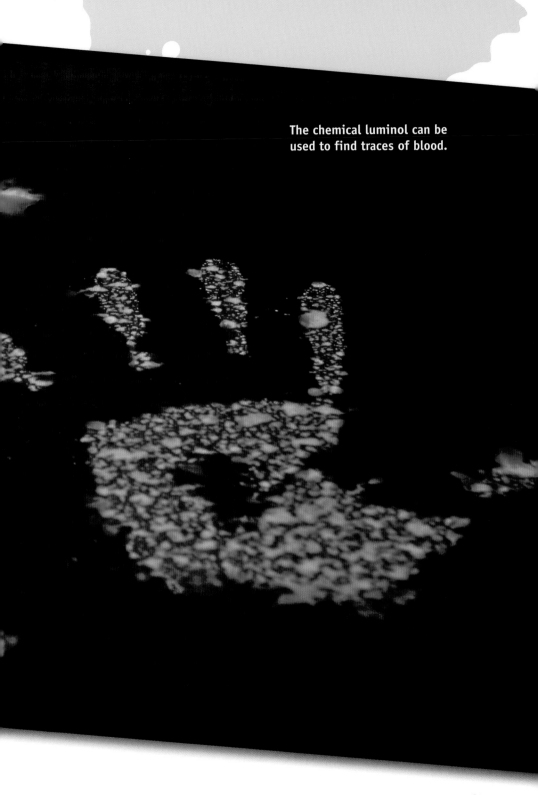

The chemical luminol can be used to find traces of blood.

and Hamilton's home, they found a large pool of blood on the floor of the bedroom. Someone had tried to clean up the blood, and had removed a section of the carpet. Investigators decided to look more closely.

To examine the area, the investigators used **luminol**, which is a chemical that can reveal faint traces of blood.[4] Luminol is prepared in a solution and sprayed on the crime scene. Blood contains tiny amounts of iron, and the iron in the blood reacts with the luminol. This reaction causes a faint blue glow that can be seen easily in the dark. This glow lasts up to half an hour. Using these techniques, investigators found more blood on the walls, door, and ceiling of the room. Samples of the blood were taken in for analysis. Based on these samples, authorities determined that the blood was Dunn's. Further, the sheer amount of the area covered by blood indicated that Dunn had lost a huge amount of blood. In fact, he had probably lost so much blood that it would have been almost impossible for him to survive whatever injuries had caused the blood loss. Based on the blood evidence, investigators were certain that Dunn had been murdered.[5]

Leisha Hamilton was an immediate suspect. Despite all the blood stains the two detectives had found in her home, Hamilton claimed that she had not noticed any blood, just the missing carpet. Not only that, but despite the fact that Dunn was her roommate and former boyfriend, she did not seem to be upset when the detectives showed her the evidence that he was dead. She had also made a phone call to Dunn's father, James, supposedly to ask him if he had seen Dunn. Over the course of the investigation, Hamilton and Dunn's father had several conversations, and Jim Dunn thought that Hamilton was acting strangely. For one thing, she seemed oddly interested in owning Scott Dunn's car. Eventually, Jim Dunn offered to give her the car when the investigation was over and Dunn's body had been found. Jim claims Hamilton looked at him and asked "What if Scott's not found in four or five years?" He told her she would have to wait.[7] These comments made her seem very suspicious, as if she knew that Dunn's body would not be found.

Police thought it was very likely that Hamilton was involved in Dunn's murder. They began investigating her, as well as her new boyfriend, Timothy Smith. It was Smith's apartment that revealed some of the most compelling evidence in the case: a roll of duct tape. Stuck to the roll of tape were a number of hairs and carpet fibers.

Hair vs. Fiber

Hair and fiber trace evidence are closely related, but they can have their own strengths

BLUESTAR AND BLEACH

Bluestar is another chemical, like luminol, that lights up in the presence of blood. Bluestar is being used more and more because the glow from the reaction is much brighter than with luminol—so bright it can be seen in the light. Bluestar also minimizes mistakes made by people interpreting the results of a test because blood reactions look a little different from the other reactions that sometimes mimic blood.

One property of both chemicals is that they not only react to blood, but they sparkle when they make contact with bleach. Bleach is often used by criminals to try and clean up blood to hide a crime. Bluestar and luminol will sparkle to reveal the bleach, telling investigators that the area has been cleaned up. Then the areas that continue glowing blue lead the investigators to the remaining blood evidence.[6]

and weaknesses. Think about what you know about these kinds of evidence. One strength of hair evidence is that it comes directly from a living being, often a suspect or victim. Hairs can sometimes be directly tied to people in ways that other fibers are not. Other fibers, however, have a different advantage. Human hairs are, in most ways, very similar. It is sometimes very difficult to tell one person's hair from another, even with a microscope. For example, fibers used to make fabrics come in a huge variety that can be obvious very quickly.

One of hair's primary advantages is that it contains DNA. According to Jarret Hallcox and Amy Welch of the National Forensic Academy, "Hair is one of the most common items used to get DNA. To get a good sample, the CSI [or crime scene investigator] needs the root. The root most often comes out at a crime scene during a struggle when hair is pulled out."[8] Because many crimes involve the victim fighting back, investigators sometimes get good hair evidence for DNA testing. However, even when using DNA evidence, hair must be compared to hairs from the victim or suspect. A piece of material, like a hair, taken to compare to a piece of evidence is called an examplar. A wide selection of hairs is generally used. Collecting hair can be unpleasant—it generally involves plucking hair from the head and various areas on the body. It may take well over a hundred hairs plucked from a person to get a match.[9] And this kind of selection is most important when dealing with microscopic analysis.

"Despite the possibility of it providing DNA evidence, hair can be treated as any other fiber," says writer N. E. Genge, author of *The Forensic Casebook*.[10] Hairs can be analyzed by a microscope, just like other fibers. As you've learned, microscopic analysis of hairs can show a difference between a number of properties in hair, including the color, the size and shape of the root, the scale pattern in the cuticle, and the structure of cells in the medulla. Hair can also be used to find medicines, drugs, and other contaminants that a person has been exposed to and have deposited into the hair. It can also be identified by the kink or twist of the hair—what has been done to it, or how naturally curly or wavy it is. Further, dyes and other hair treatments leave their mark on a person's hair. Not only can the chemicals and color used in dye be found in a hair, but the length of the undyed roots of a hair can be used to tell how long ago

KNOTS

While a lot of fiber analysis happens under a microscope, sometimes clues can be found without them. One type of evidence that fiber specialists use is knots. Unusual knots can point to people with special skills, such as sailors, firefighters, or scouts. Sometimes how the knot has been tied can indicate who tied it. Suppose a body is found strangled, as if the person had been hanged. Was it a suicide or a murder? The way the rope was tied could indicate that it had been tied by someone standing behind the person, or by a left-handed person. This can lead investigators to suspects, or make a murder seem more likely than a suicide.

the hair was dyed. A person's hair grows at a mostly constant rate. Suppose a hair is found at a crime scene. Then another hair is taken from a suspect shortly after the crime. Investigators can see if the two hairs have about the same amount of undyed root. Combined with other microscopic analysis, this fact makes it much more likely that the hairs come from the same person.

But as you've learned, when it comes to dyes and chemicals, hairs are much less likely to reveal something useful than other fibers. Almost all fibers used every day have been altered or processed in a specific way. Trace evidence specialist Jay Paresh says that some trace examination " . . . includes chemical testing that can destroy a sample. So it's the end of the analysis process, but it can give us specific formulations that, when

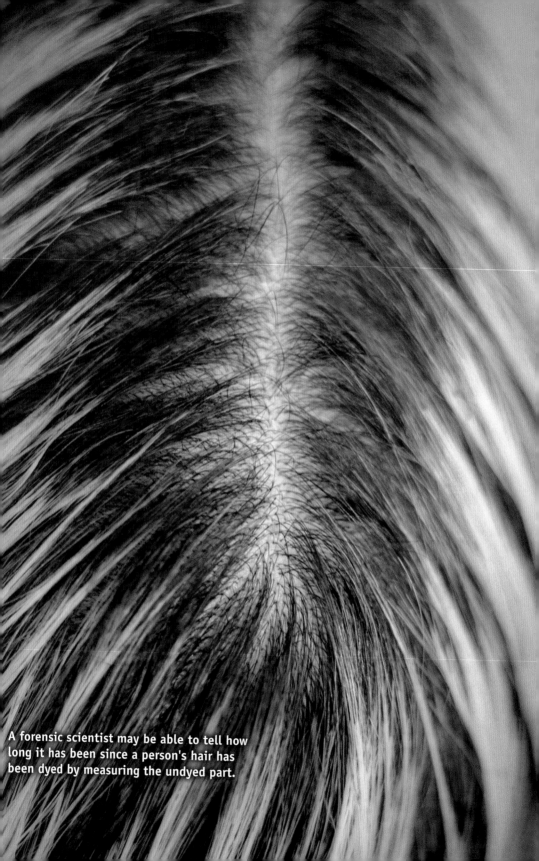

A forensic scientist may be able to tell how long it has been since a person's hair has been dyed by measuring the undyed part.

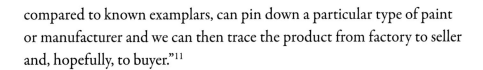

compared to known examplars, can pin down a particular type of paint or manufacturer and we can then trace the product from factory to seller and, hopefully, to buyer."[11]

Evidence That Sticks

In the case of Scott Dunn, investigators had both hair and fiber evidence to study. The hairs on the roll of tape found in Smith's apartment were consistent with hairs taken from Scott Dunn's hairbrush. Further, the carpet fibers found stuck to the tape matched the green carpeting in Dunn's apartment. Smith's carpet was grey, so there was no doubt that the fibers could not have come from his own home. Investigators had no doubt that Dunn had been murdered, and they had little doubt that Hamilton and Smith had been involved. Based on testimony from the suspects and those who knew them, investigators came up with a theory explaining how and why the murder had taken place.

Scott Dunn had been living with and dating Leisha Hamilton. However, he had recently become engaged to another woman. Hamilton was upset by this, and soon began dating Timothy Smith. According to a former boyfriend of Hamilton's, she began dating Smith with the goal of making Dunn jealous. Smith viewed Dunn as a threat to his relationship with Hamilton. Meanwhile, Hamilton was infuriated by Dunn's engagement. Hamilton encouraged Smith to kill Dunn, and together they beat him to death in the apartment Dunn and Hamilton shared. They then disposed of his body (and the missing carpet). How they got rid of the body is still unknown.[13]

A large amount of evidence worked together to support this theory. The trace blood evidence proved that Dunn had been murdered. Hamilton's odd behavior, along with testimony from witnesses, indicated that she had been involved. The hair and fiber trace evidence showed that her boyfriend, Timothy Smith, had been involved. In 1997, a jury was

CORDUROY TO CATCH A THIEF

Not all fibers are created equal. Some materials are more likely to shed fibers than others, and one of the most likely is corduroy. According to one trace analyst, "A burglar who wears corduroy is making a big mistake . . . you've got a lot of loose fibers, you've got a lot of fibers sticking up, a lot of surface area for stuff to stick to. You bring corduroy into a crime scene—it's both a big source of evidence and a big collector of evidence."[12]

presented with the evidence and the prosecutors' arguments against the two suspects. The jury found Hamilton and Smith guilty of murder. Smith was not given a jail sentence, but Hamilton had a prior criminal record and was sentenced to twenty years. And the case might never have been closed if Timothy Smith had gotten rid of a roll of tape with key evidence stuck to it.

7

The Math Behind the Science

Trace evidence is a powerful tool, but it has limitations. Fibers or footprints can make it likely a suspect was near a victim or crime scene, but they cannot usually prove that a suspect is the only one who could have been there. Fingerprints and DNA can prove a victim was in a suspect's home, but not that the victim died there. Sometimes trace evidence just is not enough to prove a suspect guilty. And sometimes the biggest weakness of trace evidence is the people using it.

In 1989, Cecil Sutherland was convicted of murder in the state of Illinois. He had been found guilty of killing Amy Schulz. Two hairs had been found on the girl's body. According to Kenneth Knight, a police scientist working on the case, the hairs were "the key in revealing the identity of Amy's killer."[1] And they were not the only evidence. There were fibers, dog hairs, and a tire track that could all potentially link

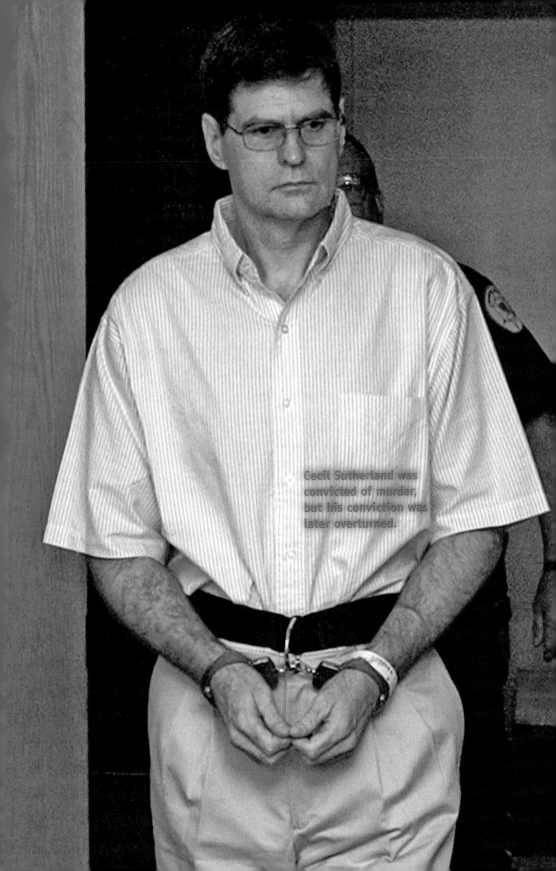

Cecil Sutherland was convicted of murder, but his conviction was later overturned.

Sutherland to the murders. With so much evidence, it is not surprising that Sutherland was found guilty.

What might surprise you is that the conviction was overturned. The Illinois Supreme Court decided that Sutherland's trial had been unfair, and decided he should have a new one. What made the trial so unfair? The prosecution in the case had overstated the quality of the trace evidence they had presented. The evidence had been enough to convince a jury that Sutherland was guilty. Unfortunately, prosecutors talked about the evidence in a way that made it seem more conclusive.

One night in 1987, Amy Schulz went out. She was looking for her brother, who was out trying to find one of the family's dogs. Schulz never returned. Her body was found the next day on an access road in the next county. The crime scene had few good clues—there were no fingerprints and no DNA that could be tested. The sheriff's office found no witnesses. The terrible crime resulted in public outrage, and the local authorities were under a lot of pressure to find the killer. They had dozens of possible suspects give hair samples to compare to the two hairs found at the crime scene. Unfortunately, they found no suspects.

Months later, Cecil Sutherland was arrested in Montana's Glacier National Park for firing a gun at passing cars. When the authorities looked into Sutherland's past, they discovered that he had once lived near the Schulz family. Sutherland pled guilty to the firearms charges against him, but became a suspect in Schulz's murder.

The trace evidence against Sutherland seemed impressive. The hairs found on Schulz's body were similar to Sutherland's. Fibers found on Schulz's body were similar to fibers found in Sutherland's car, and fibers found in Sutherland's car matched the clothes Schulz was wearing on the night she was murdered. A tire track found near the scene looked like the tread of Sutherland's car, and animal fibers found on Schulz's body appeared to come from Sutherland's dog, Babe. However, while the list of evidence was long, Sutherland's lawyers believed that none of it was very good evidence. "Certainly, we know that hair evidence, in and of itself, is not conclusive evidence. It's not like fingerprints," said Richard Bisbing, an expert who testified for the defense.[3]

However, one of the prosecutors repeatedly treated the trace evidence as if it were conclusive, or strong enough to prove something absolutely. Unfortunately, that is not really the case.

Probability

When investigators examine hairs and fibers, they deal with probability. Probability is the mathematical analysis of how likely it is that something is true. For example, when you flip a coin it is possible to calculate the probability of it

"JUNK SCIENCE"

"Junk science" is a phrase people use to describe areas of study that they believe are based on flawed information. Also called pseudoscience, junk science is a set of beliefs that people treat like science, but do not have a solid basis in fact and reason. Over the years, some people have called many aspects of trace evidence junk science—including hair analysis and the analysis of the way buildings burn to tell if a fire was set on purpose.

Good forensic scientists or trace analysts only tells a jury what they know. They may say that a burn-pattern is consistent with arson, rather than saying it proves arson. They may tell a jury that molecules on a person's hand may be from a gunshot, but it is harder to prove they actually fired a gun. They might point out that hairs on a body are similar to the hair of a victim, but it is hard to be certain it is the victim's hair. Keeping analysis limited to facts that can be proven is the best way to avoid having hard work dismissed as junk.[2]

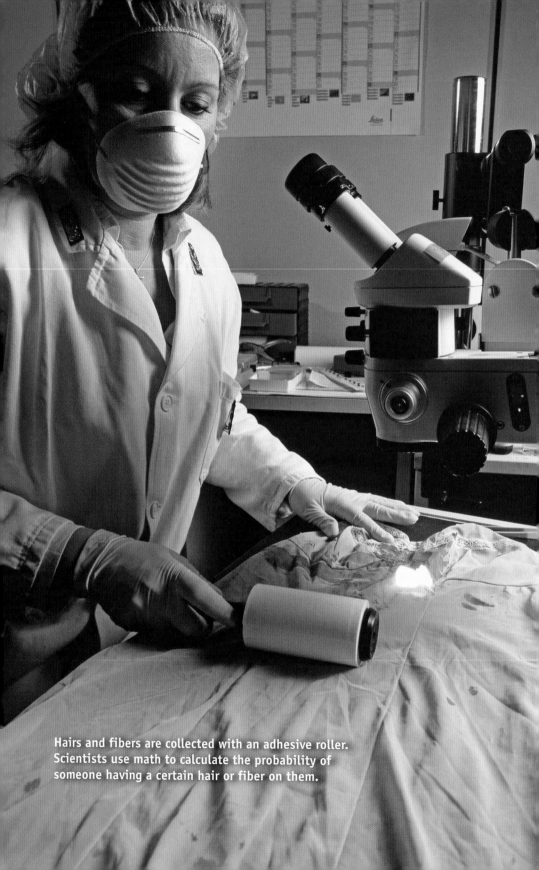

Hairs and fibers are collected with an adhesive roller. Scientists use math to calculate the probability of someone having a certain hair or fiber on them.

landing with the heads face up. If there are two possibilities, and both are equally likely, then the probability is one in two (or fifty percent).

Now suppose you want to find the probability of two flipped coins both coming up heads. Each coin has two possible outcomes. Coin 1 can come up heads (H) or tails (T). Coin 2 can also come up heads or tails. That means there are four total possible outcomes: HH, HT, TH, and TT. Whenever you want to find the total number of outcomes of unrelated events like this, you multiply the number of possible outcomes for one event by the number of possible outcomes of the other event. In this case, 2 times 2 is equal to 4. Of the four possible outcomes, in one both coins come up heads. That means the possibility is one in four (or twenty-five percent). A more complicated version of this kind of math is used in hair and fiber analysis.

Suppose you have an unusual fiber that was found on both a suspect and at a crime scene. Even if the fiber is very rare, finding it on two people does not mean they definitely met. Coincidences do happen, even very unlikely ones. If an analyst calculates the odds of someone having that particular fiber found on them at one in a thousand (or 0.1%), at first that may make it seem very unlikely you can find anyone other than the suspect who will have the fiber on them. But imagine for a moment that a murder takes place in a large city with a population of a million. In a city of that size, a thousand people could have the fiber found on them! No matter how unlikely something seems, unless it is impossible there will be some doubt.

Probability even has to be judged in cases where DNA is matched. The field of population **genetics** is the science of determining how often certain genetic traits appear, particularly in humans. Some genetic traits—like a person's blood type—might be quite common. Other traits are much rarer. And when many traits are looked at together, it quickly becomes very unlikely that any two people will share all the same traits.[4]

POPULATION GENETICS

Population genetics studies genetic variability within a group. Generally, it's good for a group—such as humans—to have variation in their genes. If all members of a species had exactly the same genes, they would all be virtually identical—and they would all have the same strengths and weaknesses. This makes it harder for the group to adapt to change. Think of a group's genes like a toolbox. If everyone had the same genes, it would be like having a toolbox full of nothing but hammers. If things change, we would want as many tools as possible to survive the change. Suppose a new disease appears. Some people may be more resistant to the disease than others because of their genes. Different people might be resistant to different diseases. If everyone's genes were identical, everyone would be vulnerable to the same diseases. That would mean a dangerous disease could threaten the entire species! Being a little bit different makes it harder for one danger to threaten all of us.

The question facing juries in criminal trials is whether or not a doubt is reasonable. If hair or fiber evidence is found as evidence against a suspect, juries must decide if the probability that the suspect is guilty is so great that their doubts are unreasonable. If a fiber is unusual enough that one in a hundred people might have the fiber on them, a juror might decide they can reasonably doubt that a suspect is guilty because many other people might have that fiber on them. However, take the case of DNA evidence. In that case, the odds of someone else having the same DNA may be one in a trillion. That means it is almost impossible that someone else has the same DNA, and doubts may be unreasonable.

Whether a juror decides his or her doubts are

reasonable or not depends not only on the math, but also on what the prosecutors say about the math. Not everyone understands how these complicated calculations work, so juries rely on what they hear about it during the trial. If you do not know much about a subject, you rely on experts to help you form a opinion. Juries usually trust a prosecutor, so the prosecutor's arguments play an important part in determining whether a suspect is found guilty or not guilty.

An Unfair Trial?

When co-prosecutor Matthew Schneider discussed the trace evidence found in the Sutherland case, he left out some important information. This may have made the trial unfair. The forensic experts in the case testified that the hairs found "could have" been from the suspect. They said that the dog hairs "could have" been from the family dog. They also claimed that the fibers "could have" been from Schulz's clothes. All of this evidence "could have" connected Sutherland to the crime. But when Schneider made his arguments, he left out the words "could have." For example, he stated that fibers from Schulz's clothes were found in Sutherland's car when he should have said that fibers that could have been from Schulz's clothes were found in Sutherland's car. He even stated that hair and fiber evidence was an "exact science"—when, in fact, it is a science based on probability, not exact certainty.[5]

This is what made the Illinois Supreme Court think that the trial was unfair. Sutherland was being sentenced to die when the evidence against him was not certain. Sutherland's mother once said, "How can you do what they're doing to him when the best you got is maybe?"[6] Yet the jury was being told that the evidence was stronger than it was. The Illinois Supreme Court thought that the jury was being misled. And the jury certainly seemed to believe that the evidence was certain. "They told us that hair matched. They said the fibers matched," one juror said.[7]

BURDEN OF PROOF

The phrase "burden of proof" is used to describe which side in an argument or debate has the responsibility to prove something is true. In the United States criminal justice system, a suspect is innocent until proven guilty. That means that the burden of proof is on the prosecutors. In order for prosecutors to win the argument and convict a suspect, they must prove the person guilty. The suspect does not have to prove his innocence; he only has to prove that he might be innocent.

"It was real clear-cut: the hair, fiber, the tire track. Each pointed to him," said another.[8] Clearly, at least one jury member believed the trace evidence was very clear, even though it was somewhat uncertain. The courts believed the trial was unfair. The prosecutor's misstatements might have allowed Sutherland to go free—even though he was found guilty.

More than a decade after his initial conviction, Sutherland went to trial again. In the time since his first trial, the science of DNA testing had improved. When Sutherland got his second trial, there was actually much stronger evidence against him.[9] Because of much more precise evidence in the form of DNA testing, Sutherland was convicted for a second time—and this time, the conviction was based on fair, accurate arguments.

Serving Justice

n 1992, Kyle Unger was sent to prison to serve a life sentence. He had been convicted of the murder of Brigitte Grenier in Manitoba, Canada. The key piece of evidence in his case had been a hair found on Grenier's body. That hair helped to send Unger to prison. More than thirteen years later the same hair would set Unger free.

Brigitte Grenier attended the Woodstick Music Festival at a ski resort in 1990. That night, she was assaulted and murdered. Her body was found in a nearby creek the next day. Five days later, authorities arrested two suspects: Kyle Unger and Timothy Houlahan. Houlahan claimed that he had been present at the murder, but that Unger had actually killed the girl. (Houlahan later gave a conflicting account, saying they both had killed Grenier). A single hair found on Grenier's body seemed to back up his story. Investigators used the process of hair microscopy to determine that the hair could have come from Kyle Unger. The hair alone would not be enough to convict Unger of the murder, but investigators had two other pieces of compelling evidence. First, they had Houlahan's testimony that he and Unger had killed the girl

Kyle Unger (right) was wrongfully sent to prison based on hair evidence. Years later, he was released using the same evidence.

together. Second, Unger had actually confessed to the killing. Though he denied any involvement all through his trial, when he had been approached by undercover police officers he had claimed to have killed Grenier. With a hair, an informant, and even a confession, it was not difficult for a jury to find both Unger and Houlahan guilty. They were sentenced to life in prison.[1]

There was only one problem: Kyle Unger was probably innocent.

The three key pieces of evidence in the case against Kyle Unger were an eyewitness account, a confession, and a matching hair. As it turned out, each of those pieces of evidence was misleading. First, the eyewitness in the case was also a suspect. Because Houlahan once claimed that Unger had done the actual killing of the girl, it was possible that he was lying to try to shift

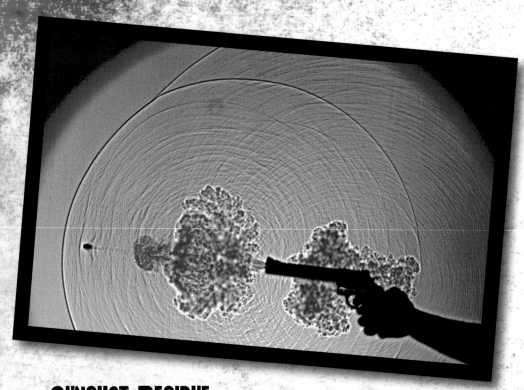

GUNSHOT RESIDUE

One kind of trace evidence that has faced legal challenges in recent years is gunshot residue evidence. When a person fires a gun, some chemicals in the gun are released in a cloud of gas. Some of these chemicals are unique to gunfire, so if someone has these chemicals on their hands it is a good indication that they fired a gun.

The problem with this kind of evidence is that the chemicals from the gunshot spread very easily. "The ability to contaminate is the reason that there is such a limited degree of conclusions that can be made with gunshot residue," said gunshot residue expert Marc S. Taylor.[2] In other words, because the chemicals from a gunshot get everywhere very easily it is hard to say that someone with those chemicals on their hands actually fired a gun. Some districts are adopting new procedures to try to make sure tests for gunshot residue work. However, there are still many worries that people have been sent to prison based on flawed gunshot residue tests.

blame from himself. Houlahan's own conviction was overturned after he appealed. He committed suicide before he could be given a new trial, and now we will never know for certain why he told the police that he had killed Grenier.

The second piece of evidence was Unger's confession. Though Unger was arrested shortly after the murder, he was originally released due to lack of evidence. However, police still suspected he was involved. They decided to set up a sting, a plan to go undercover and talk to Unger until he confessed. Police officers contacted Unger claiming to be drug dealers. They hinted to him that they would offer him a job if he told them he'd murdered Grenier. Unger confessed to the murder, and the police arrested him.

However, many people thought that this confession could not be trusted. Unger had never told anyone else that he had killed Grenier. Further, by saying that they would offer him a job for confessing, police had given Unger a reason to lie: ". . . along come some fellows who say all you've got to do is admit to something, and we'll give you a job, we'll give you money, you'll have friends, so there's an **inducement** there, and people have been known to lie when there's an inducement," said Alan Libman, a spokesperson for the Association in Defence of the Wrongly Convicted.[3] In his trial, Unger claimed he had lied to the "drug dealers" to impress them. This seems like it was probably the truth, because Unger's confession actually had many of the facts of the case wrong. He claimed that he had thrown the murder weapon away, even though the weapon had not been thrown away. He also claimed that he had committed the murder on a bridge, even though the bridge in that area had actually been built after the murder. Kyle Unger may not have been a murderer after all—maybe he was just a liar.

It was not hard to believe that Houlahan lied. A jury might even believe that Unger lied in his confession. However, that still left the hair that had been found on Grenier's body. Could that have lied as well? As science advances, tools for solving crimes advance with it. Just like computers today are faster than the first computers were, modern DNA evidence is much more reliable than hair microscopy. In the case of Kyle Unger, authorities in the early 1990s had not used DNA testing on the hair found on Grenier's body. What could modern technology reveal?

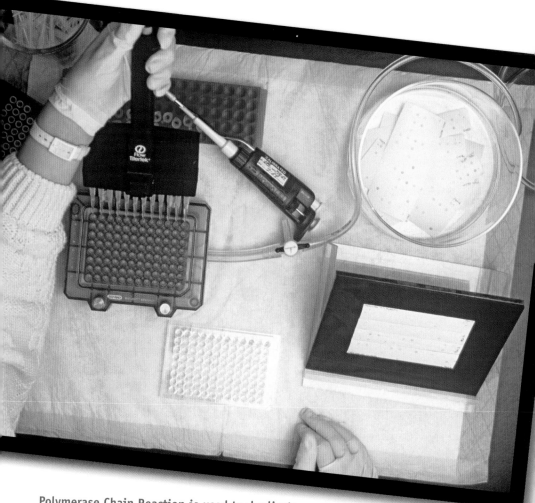

Polymerase Chain Reaction is used to duplicate DNA in order to create a larger sample.

DNA ERRORS

Even though DNA science has become very advanced, there are still errors in DNA analysis. According to Jarret Hallcox and Amy Welch of the National Forensic Academy, "Tragically, poor procedures and standards at DNA laboratories have helped prosecute the innocent at an alarming rate by improperly sequencing a suspect's DNA."[4] Sometimes DNA is contaminated by cells from other people at the crime scene. The forensic scientists themselves could accidentally let their own DNA contaminate a sample. No matter how effective scientific techniques become, there is always the possibility of human error.

Advances in DNA Analysis

There are many different ways to perform DNA analysis, but two of the most important are **Restriction Fragment Length Polymorphism** (RFLP) and the **Polymerase Chain Reaction** (PCR). RFLP analysis was the first DNA matching technique that was inexpensive enough that it could be used by many different investigators. It isn't used as much anymore because newer techniques have many advantages. PCR is the basis for a number of newer techniques, including some of the most effective forms of modern DNA analysis.[5]

PCR analysis finds a small piece of DNA and uses **enzymes** to make millions and millions of copies of it. This means that PCR can be used even when there is very little DNA present. Instead of fifteen hairs,

DNA could be collected from a single hair. It could even be collected from a drop of saliva!

Today, there are newer techniques based on PCR. Because the DNA is duplicated rather than destroyed, analysts can potentially perform tests over and over again on the same sample. PCR has another advantage as well. Because the pieces of DNA replicated are small, the technique works even when the DNA has been damaged. As long as the DNA has not been so damaged that the tiny pieces used in PCR are damaged as well, the PCR technique will work on DNA that is old or has been exposed to sunlight and heat for a long time. DNA is fairly tough, but with PCR techniques it can be used even when it's been broken into pieces.

Because of the advantages of the PCR technique, it is now used in a huge variety of fields. It is used in medicine to help diagnose genetic diseases. It is used in zoology to analyze the DNA of ancient animals. And it is now used routinely in testing DNA evidence in criminal cases.

Setting Innocent People Free

Kyle Unger was convicted in the Canadian province of Manitoba. In 2003, the province decided to conduct a review of murder cases involving hair evidence. Because hair evidence can be less specific than DNA, investigators decided to use new DNA technology to recheck many of the cases where hair evidence had been used. Kyle Unger's case was one of the cases reviewed. When DNA testing was conducted on the hair found on Grenier's body, it was discovered that the hair was not Unger's after all. The original analysis had misled prosecutors and the jury. After more than thirteen years in prison, Unger was released on bail to await a new trial. In 2009, prosecutors decided to drop the charges against Unger due to a lack of evidence. According to prosecutor Dan Slough, new tests "did not find any trace of Unger on the victim."[6]

Unger's case and others have cast doubt on the use of traditional hair analysis in trials. However, as DNA evidence advances, hairs can become even more important in identifying criminals and ruling out suspects that are not guilty. The Innocence Project is an organization dedicated to helping to free wrongfully convicted people using DNA testing. As of 2010, 261 people in the United States have been freed from prison because of new DNA evidence. According to the Innocence Project, "DNA testing has been a major factor in changing the criminal justice system. It has provided scientific proof that our system convicts and sentences innocent people—and that wrongful convictions are not isolated or rare events."[7]

STR

One of the best methods for modern DNA analysis is called Short Tandem Repeats, or STR. STR is based on the PCR technique. The PCR process that multiplies bits of DNA is used on specific pieces of DNA that are very different from person to person. Because these bits of DNA rarely match, the tests differentiate very effectively between different people. The likelihood of DNA from two people who are not identical twins being matched using STR analysis can be as low as one in a quintillion. That's like three one-in-a-million coincidences in a row!

It is important to remember that trace evidence is only as good as the people using it. Trace evidence is based on proven science, but people do not always remember that that science is based on probability. Trace evidence can be vital to finding leads and convicting criminals, but it can also be misused. Fortunately, the use of DNA evidence has made many investigations much more certain. Trace evidence may never be perfect. However, as science progresses, trace analysts will find new ways to use trace evidence to serve justice.

CAREERS

CRIME LAB DIRECTOR

Job Description: Lead, guide, and assist laboratory technicians. Act as a liaison between the laboratory and law enforcement. Review the laboratory budget and oversee the training of new employees.

Education Required: Bachelor's degree in natural science; Some labs require a higher degree such as a master's degree or a PhD.

Average Salary: $58,000–$125,000

CRIME SCENE INVESTIGATOR

Job Description: Responsible for collecting, documenting, and processing evidence found at a crime scene. The CSI acts as support for the investigator for a case.

Education Required: Varies by location—some agencies may require a two- or four-year degree, while others may not require a degree.

Average Salary: $20,000–$50,000

CRIME LAB TECHNICIAN

Job Description: Collect, identify, and analyze evidence related to crimes. Test weapons or evidence to determine relevance to an investigation.

Education Required: Bachelor's degree in a natural science

Average Salary: $40,000

CRIMINOLOGIST

Job Description: Analyze the behaviors and methods of criminals to predict, prevent, and solve crimes.

Education Required: Bachelor's degree in psychology, sociology, or criminal science; Some criminologists have master's degrees or PhDs.

Average Salary: $30,000–$55,000

DNA ANALYST

Job Description: **Perform DNA analysis on evidence to determine relevance to an investigation.**

Education Required: **Bachelor's degree in a natural science**

Average Salary: **$54,000–$76,000**

FORENSIC ANTHROPOLOGIST

Job Description: **Help identify human remains.**

Education Required: **Forensic anthropologists usually earn a PhD in anthropology.**

Average Salary: **$54,000**

FORENSIC PATHOLOGIST

Job Description: **Investigate the time, manner, and cause of death by collecting samples and conducting an autopsy on a body.**

Education Required: **Bachelor's degree, medical degree (MD)**

Average Salary: **$80,000–$120,000**

TRACE ANALYST

Job Description: **Help investigate crimes and road accidents involving trace evidence like hairs and fibers, paint, glass, soil, and arson residue.**

Education Required: **Bachelor's degree in chemistry or other natural science. Microscope experience and extensive training may also be necessary.**

Average Salary: **$24,000–$36,000**

CHAPTER NOTES

CHAPTER 1. PUTTING PIECES TOGETHER

1. Sir Arthur Conan Doyle, *The Complete Sherlock Holmes, Volume 1* (New York: Doubleday, 1927), p. 324.

2. Connie Fletcher, *Every Contact Leaves a Trace* (New York: St. Martin's Press, 2006), p. 135.

3. Doyle, p. 190.

4. E.J. Wagner, *The Science of Sherlock Holmes* (Hoboken, N.J.: John Wiley & Sons, 2006), p. 77.

5. Wagner, p. 79.

6. Paule Leland Kirk, *Crime Investigation: Physical Evidence and the Police Laboratory* (New York: Interscience Publishers, 1953), p. 4.

7. Fletcher, p. 137.

8. Suzanne Bell, *The Facts on File Dictionary of Forensic Science* (New York: Checkmark Books, 2004), p. 87.

9. Norah Rudin and Keith Inman, "Forensic Science Timeline," *Forensicdna.com,* February 7, 2002, <http://www.forensicdna.com/Timeline020702.pdf> (December 5, 2009).

10. Fletcher, p. 135.

11. Wagner, p. 79.

12. Fletcher, p. 138.

CHAPTER 2. COMBING FOR EVIDENCE

1. Katherine Ramsland, "Trace Evidence: Fiber Analysis," *Crime Library on TruTV.com,* n.d., <http://www.trutv.com/library/crime/criminal_mind/forensics/trace/3.html> (December 5, 2009).

2. Jarrett Hallcox and Amy Welch, *Bodies We've Buried* (New York: Berkley Books, 2006), p. 233.

3. Fletcher, p. 149.

4. Douglas W. Deedrick, "Hairs, Fibers, Crime, and Evidence," *Forensic Science Communications*, July 2000, <http://www.fbi.gov/hq/lab/fsc/backissu/july2000/deedric3.htm#Natural%20Fibers> (December 5, 2009).

5. Brian M. Tissue, "Spectroscopy," *Chemistry Hypermedia Project,* 2000, <http://www.files.chem.vt.edu/chem-ed/spec/spectros.html> (December 5, 2009).

6. Deedrick.

7. James Renner, *The Serial Killer's Apprentice* (Ohio: Gray and Company, 2008), pp. 223–224.

CHAPTER 3. NOT QUITE SPOTLESS

1. Connie Fletcher, *Every Contact Leaves a Trace* (New York: St. Martin's Press, 2006), p. 146.

2. Jarrett Hallcox and Amy Welch, *Behind the Yellow Tape* (New York: Berkley Books, 2009), p. 98.

3. Fletcher, p. 139.

4. Ibid., p. 148.

5. Ibid., p. 145.

6. Ibid., pp. 139–140.

7. Hallcox and Welch, p. 101.

8. Ibid., p. 101.

CHAPTER 4. WHEN IS TRACE EVIDENCE MEANINGFUL?

1. Marilyn Bardsley and Rachael Bell, "The Atlanta Child Murders," *Crime Library on TruTV.com,* n.d., <http://www.trutv.com/ library/crime/serial_killers/predators/williams/trial_12.html> (December 5, 2009).

2. Ibid.

3. John W. Hicks, *Microscopy of Hairs: A Practical Guide and Manual* (Washington, D.C.: Federal Bureau of Investigation, 1977), p. 6.

4. Bardsley and Bell.

5. Ibid.

CHAPTER 5. PILING ON THE EVIDENCE

1. "Westerfield guilty of Danielle van Dam's murder," *Cnn.com/Law Center*, August 27, 2002, <http://archives.cnn.com/2002/ LAW/08/21/westerfield.trial/index.html> (December 5, 2009).

2. Judge Gerald Sheindlin, *Genetic Fingerprinting: The Law and Science of DNA* (Bethel, Conn.: Rutledge Books, 1996), p. 46.

3. Connie Fletcher, *Every Contact Leaves a Trace* (New York: St. Martin's Press, 2006), p. 137–138.

4. Ibid.

5. Harriet Ryan, "Criminalist: Fibers in RV similar to those in van Dam home," *Cnn.com/Law Center*. June 25, 2002, <http:// archives.cnn.com/2002/LAW/06/25/ctv.westerfield.trial/index. html> (December 5, 2009).

6. "Criminalist: Blond Hairs On Westerfield Bed Sheets," *10news. com*, June 24, 2002, <http://www.10news.com/news/1527754/ detail.html> (December 5, 2009).

7. *Cnn.com/Law Center*.

8. Ibid.

9. "Van Dam Parents Prepare for Sad Birthday," *ABC News*, March 27, 2006, <http://abcnews.go.com/Primetime/story?id=132078&page=1&page=1> (December 5, 2009).

CHAPTER 6. VANISHED WITH A TRACE

1. Graham Underwood, "Bloodstains Focus of Trial," *Avalanche-Journal*, May 13, 1997, <http://www.lubbockonline.com/news/051497/bloodsta.htm> (December 5, 2009).

2. "Roger Scott Dunn," *The Charley Project*. May 9, 2008, <http://www.charleyproject.org/cases/d/dunn_roger.html> (December 5, 2009).

3. Underwood.

4. "Roger Scott Dunn."

5. Ibid.

6. Jarrett Hallcox and Amy Welch, *Behind the Yellow Tape* (New York: Berkley Books, 2009), p. 230.

7. Underwood.

8. Jarrett Hallcox and Amy Welch, *Bodies We've Buried* (New York: Berkley Books, 2006), p. 230.

9. N. E. Genge, *The Forensic Casebook* (New York: Ballantine Books, 2002), p. 93.

10. Ibid.

11. Ibid., p. 84.

12. Connie Fletcher, *Every Contact Leaves a Trace* (New York: St. Martin's Press, 2006), pp. 148–149.

13. "Roger Scott Dunn."

CHAPTER 7. THE MATH BEHIND THE SCIENCE

1. Steve Mills and Ken Armstrong, "The Failure of the Death Penalty in Illinois—Part 5: Convicted by a Hair," *ChicagoTribune.com,* November 18, 1999, <http://www.chicagotribune.com/news/watchdog/chi-991118deathillinois5,0,196862.story> (December 5, 2009).

2. Stephanie Hanes, "Evidence Under Suspicion," *The Baltimore Sun*, January 23, 2005.

3. Mills and Armstrong.

4. Judge Gerald Sheindlin, *Genetic Fingerprinting: The Law and Science of DNA* (Bethel, Conn.: Rutledge Books, 1996), p. 62.

5. Mills and Armstrong.

6. Ibid.

7. Ibid.

8. Ibid.

9. "Jury finds Sutherland guilty—now facing death penalty," *KVS12 News,* June 14, 2004, <http://lists.washlaw.edu/pipermail/deathpenalty/2004-June/000145.html> (December 5, 2009).

CHAPTER 8. SERVING JUSTICE

1. "Timeline: What happened to Kyle Wayne Unger?" *Winnipeg Free Press,* October 24, 2009, <http://www.winnipegfreepress.com/local/What-happened-to-Kyle-Wayne-Unger.html> (December 5, 2009).

2. Stephanie Hanes, "Evidence Under Suspicion," *The Baltimore Sun*, January 23, 2005.

3. "Unger leaves jail, murder conviction under review," *CTV News,* November 24, 2005, <http://www.ctv.ca/servlet/ArticleNews/story/CTVNews/20051124/kyle_unger_release_051124/20051124?hub=Canada> (December 5, 2009).

4. Jarrett Hallcox and Amy Welch, *Behind the Yellow Tape* (New York: Berkley Books, 2009), p. 259.

5. Judge Gerald Sheindlin, *Genetic Fingerprinting: The Law and Science of DNA* (Bethel, Conn.: Rutledge Books, 1996), p. 59.

6. "Canada: Kyle Unger Acquitted Of Murder After 14 Years In Jail," *The Huffington Post,* October 23, 2009, <http://www.huffingtonpost.com/2009/10/23/canada-kyle-unger-acquitt_n_331750.html> (December 5, 2009).

7. "About the Innocence Project," *The Innocence Project Mission Statement*, n.d., <http://www.innocenceproject.org/about/> (December 11, 2010).

GLOSSARY

circumstantial evidence—Evidence that indirectly proves a fact.

contaminate—To make dirty or impure.

cortex—The layer of hair underneath the cuticle, made of coiled proteins.

criminologist—A person who studies crimes and criminal behavior.

cuticle—The outer layer of a hair, which has cells arranged like roof shingles.

deoxyribonucleic acid (DNA)—A molecule found in all living cells. It carries information about a living thing, such as a person's hair or eye color.

entomology—The study of insects.

enzyme—A special molecule that speeds up a chemical reaction in the body.

forensic science—The use of different types of science to solve crimes or the use of natural science in matter of the law.

genetics—The study of how parents pass traits on to their children through their genes.

inducement—A reason to do something given by someone else, such as a bribe.

keratin—A tough type of protein. Human hairs and fingernails are made of keratin.

luminol—A chemical that forensic scientists use to find traces of blood.

medulla—The inner core of some hairs, made of cells that can be arranged in patterns.

modus operandi—A criminal's typical method of committing a crime.

Polymerase Chain Reaction (PCR)—A type of DNA analysis that works by making millions and millions of copies of a piece of DNA.

Restriction Fragment Length Polymorphism (RFLP)—A type of DNA analysis that works by separating DNA into parts and organizing them by size.

search warrant—A legal document allowing police to search an area.

spectrophotometry—A method of identifying substances by testing how they react to light.

synthetic—A material made of chemicals. Man-made fibers, like polyester, are synthetic.

trace evidence—Evidence that is often small or partial, such as hairs, fibers, fingerprints, residue, glass, paint chips, and other materials that may be found at a crime scene.

FURTHER READING

BOOKS

Adams, Bradley J. *Forensic Anthropology*. New York: Chelsea House, 2007.

Allman, Toney. *The Medical Examiner*. Detroit: Lucent Books, 2006.

Davis, Barbara J. *In the Laboratory*. Milwaukee: World Almanac Library, 2007.

Hunter, William. *Mark and Trace Analysis*. Philadelphia: Mason Crest Publishers, 2006.

Jeffrey, Gary. *Solving Crimes with Trace Evidence*. New York: Rosen Central, 2008.

Wright, John D. *Hair and Fibers*. Armonk, N.Y.: Sharpe Focus, 2008.

INTERNET ADDRESSES

Crime Lab
  <http://www.sciencenewsforkids.org/articles/20041215/
    Feature1.asp>

Cyberbee.com. Who Dunnit?
  <http://www.cyberbee.com/whodunnit/crime.htm>

Discovery Channel: Crimes and Forensics
  <http://www.yourdiscovery.com/crime/criminalists/index.shtml>

INDEX

A

amino acids, 53, 55
animal hair, 45, 46
Atlanta child murders, 39–42, 46–50

B

ballistics, 12
bleach, 63
blood evidence, 51, 55–56, 60–63
bloodstain pattern analysis, 12, 33, 36–37
Bluestar, 63
Buell, Robert, 27–28
burden of proof, 78
Bureau of Criminal Identification and Investigation (BCI), 27

C

careers, 90–91
cars, vehicles, 29–37
Cater, Nathaniel, 42
cell structure, 56
circumstantial evidence, 38–39, 50–51
color analysis (spectrophotometry), 25
confessions, 36–37, 59, 83, 85
cordage, 22
corduroy, 68
cortex of hair, 42
crime lab director, 90
crime lab technician, 90
crime scene investigator, 90

criminologists, 8, 90
cross-section of objects, 23
cuticle of hair, 42, 64

D

DNA analysts, 91
DNA evidence
    advances in, 87–88
    evidence reexamination, 89
    in hair, 14–16, 53, 64
    overview, 12, 52–56
    probability and, 76
    reliability of, 86, 87
Doyle, Arthur Conan, 7, 8
Dunn, Scott, 59–63, 67–69
dyes, 26

E

entomology, 57
evidence
    blood, 51, 55–56, 60–63
    circumstantial, 38–39, 50–51
    contamination, 21, 65, 84
    DNA (*see* DNA evidence)
    fiber (*see* fiber evidence)
    hair (*see* hair evidence)
    impression, 32
    trace, 10–14, 70
examplars, 64
eyewitness testimony, 30–32

F

fiber analysis, 12
fiber analysts, 21

fiber evidence
corduroy, 68
hair *vs.,* 63–67
limitations of, 77–79
natural, 23
overview, 21–27
probability and, 75, 76
synthetic, 23, 27
van Dam murder, 56–57
field kits, 17
fingerprints, 11, 12, 57
follicles of hair, 43
Fontaine mystery, 10, 16–18
footprints, 16, *34*
forensic anthropologist, 91
forensic entomology, 57
forensic pathologist, 91
forensic science, 10–12

G
Goddard, Henry, 12
Grenier, Brigitte, 81–86, 88
Gross, Hans, 8
gunshot residue, 84

H
hair analysts, 45, 46
hair dyes, 64–65
hair evidence
animal, 45, 46
DNA in, 14–16, 53, 64
fiber *vs.,* 63–67
limitations of, 77–79, 81, 88–89
overview, 42–46
probability and, 76
Schulz murder, 70–73
van Dam murder, 56–57

Hamilton, Leisha, 60, 62–63, 67–69
Harrison, Krista, 19, 27–28
Holmes, Sherlock, 7–8
Houlahan, Timothy, 81–86

I
impression evidence, 32
inducements, 85
infrared light, 26
Innocence Project, 89

J
Jones, Clifford, 49
junk science, 73

K
keratin, 42
knots, 65

L
Lee, Henry, 32
light spectrum, 25, 26
linking crimes, 39
Locard, Edmond, 12
Locard's exchange principle, 12
luminol, 62, 63

M
mammals, 42
medulla of hair, 42, 45, 64
modus operandi (MO), 39

N
natural fibers, 23

P
paint, 32–33
PDQ (Paint Data Query), 33
plastic evidence, 27

polymerase chain reaction (PCR), 87–88

population genetics, 75–76

pressure washers, 36

probability, 73–77

R

reasonable doubt, 40, 55–58, 76–77

restriction fragment length polymorphism (RFLP), 87

S

saliva, 53

Schrieffer, Erik, 29–30, 33–37

Schulz, Amy, 70–73, 77–79

Scotland Yard, 12

search warrants, 28

Smith, Timothy, 63, 67–69

spectrophotometry (color analysis), 25

static electricity, 21

static lift, 21

Sutherland, Cecil, 70–73, 77–79

synthetic fibers, 23, 27

T

tape, 21

tire tracks, 33

Toms, John, 12

trace analyst, 91

trace evidence generally, 10–14, 70

tree bark, 14

U

ultraviolet light, 26

Unger, Kyle, 81–86, 88

V

van Dam, Danielle, 51, 55–58

vehicles, 29–37

victim identification, 46

Vidocq, Eugène François, 8–10, 16–18

W

Wehmanen, Joseph, 30, 33–37

Westerfield, David, 51, 55–58

Williams, Wayne, 39–42, 46–50

wool, 47